/\/\/\/\/\/\/\/\/\/\/\/\/\/\/\/\

Grand Bahama Island
FREEPORT NOTEBOOK

PINES, PORT, POLITICS, POEMS AND PROSE
/\

PETER J. H. BARRATT

DELIABOOKS

Copyright ©2011, Peter Barratt, Grand Bahama Island Freeport Notebook: Pines, Ports, Politics, Poems and Prose. All rights reserved.

ISBN: 978-0-9832721-3-7   (paperback)
Library of Congress Control Number: 2011932036
Copyright information available upon request.

Front cover photos (top from left): Sir Albert Miller, Edward St George, Garnet Levarity, D K Ludwig, Rt. Hon. Hubert Ingraham, PM. Centre: Wallace Groves, Sir Jack Hayward, Sir Lynden Pindling (former PM). Back cover (from left): Hannes Babak, Sir Stafford Sands, Maurice Moore (former MP for Freeport).

Interior design: J. L. Saloff
Typography: Adobe Jenson Pro, American Typewriter, Courier New, Dakota, Geometric, Humanist, InaiMathi, Square Meal, Tekton Pro.

All photographs and illustrations are the copyright of the author except for the rum runner era photograph of West End by Hix C. Stuart and the photographic reproduction of the Lucayan Canoists painting by Alton Lowe. Some of the portrait photos of local personalities were obtained from the *Freeport News* and the *Nassau Guardian*. The author has made every effort to trace the copyright holders but if any have been inadvertently over-looked, the author will be pleased to make the necessary arrangements to correct the oversight at the first opportunity.

Under copyright all rights reserved. No part of this publication may be used, reproduced in any manner, stored in a retrieval system, or transmitted in any form or by any other means, electronic, mechanical, photocopying or otherwise, without the written permission of the publisher, except in the case of brief quotations embodied in critical articles or reviews, except as may be expressly permitted by the 1976 Copyright Act or in writing by the publisher.

v. 1.0
First Edition, 2011
Printed on acid-free paper.

Copies of this book are obtainable online at Amazon,
Barnes & Noble and other fine bookstores
or in the Bahamas at islandplan@yahoo.com

DELIABOOKS

Dedicated to the people of Freeport, past and present, who made the dream of Wallace Groves come true.

Also by Peter Barratt:

Bahama Saga
(AuthorHouse)

Grand Bahama
(Macmillan, David and Charles Publishers/
Stackpole Books and I M Publishing)

Angelic Verses
(DeliaBooks)

The Port at War
(DeliaBooks)

CONTENTS

FOREWORD 1

HISTORY 3

LETTERS 69

PLANNING 93

PORT AND POLITICS 103

POEMS 125

ECONOMICS 133

PERSONALITIES 139

MISCELLANIA 153

FUTURE 171

INDEX 173

Freeport genesis—dredging underway at the mouth of Hawksbill Creek c.1955. Note centre right, Lumber Company wagons on the rail line (now part of Government Road).

FOREWORD

This is a short collection of letters, notes, insights and verses based on the life and times of Freeport, Grand Bahama spanning my over 40 years of association with the community. It includes what I call poems—though some might call them doggerel. Hopefully however, some of the verses and prose offer insights for both residents and visitors into the Grand Bahamian way of life, its politics and anomalies. Some of the prose and poems (or doggerel if you prefer), have been rendered in the local idiomatic speech common in some Bahamian conversation. Also included in this anthology are some probably never-seen-before photographs of the early years in Freeport.

There is certainly miscellany in this very personal collection. I have included some letters and prose written by myself and have plagiarized (in the nicest sense of the word) work by others that I consider is relevant to the Grand Bahamian scene. I share some very personal experiences from almost a lifetime spent in Freeport and make a comment or two about the heady time of Bahamian Independence. However sympathetic we expatriates may have been to the cause of independence we were hardly its principal beneficiaries. Indeed I bring attention to the many non-Bahamians who suffered hardship because of the political and social change that it brought.

Interestingly in this period I lost my Work Permit (twice) without any seemingly good reason and only my love of the Islands and the fact that my wife still had a business that was slowly faltering (due to the political and economic situation) drove me to stay. Many years later, some spent in exile in Miami, I was privileged to be granted Bahamian citizenship.

Oh, just a final word. One has to have an untidy mind for this kind of writing. What follows are simply very personal subjective musings that I thought the reader might find interesting. Most people familiar with Freeport are too young to know first-hand many of the situations I refer to in the text so that is why I thought it might be of interest to highlight some events in the early period in the Freeport story.

Peter Barratt
March 2011

HISTORY

If you want to hide something from your fellow man's look then in the Bahamas—put it in a book...

A Bahamian proverb (hopefully there are exceptions!)

Transcript of a Talk About the Book 'Grand Bahama'

The following is from a talk given at Books & Books in Coral Gables to promote the third edition of the book 'Grand Bahama.' Hopefully it gives historical context and background to the island.

I am often asked why I wrote a book about Grand Bahama. One reason of course is that nobody else had... but another is that years ago an author of a glossy publication on the island said Grand Bahama had no history!

Well of course everywhere has history! Whether it is interesting or not—that is really the question ...and a challenge for a would-be historian. My book came out of the background research I was undertaking on the island after being appointed Town Planner in Freeport in 1964. I felt it would have been wrong to limit my research just to Freeport since the influence of Freeport is felt—in varying degrees—all over the island.

Since the book stands or falls on its merits I will let you be the judge. So now I will try to cover some matters that are not mentioned in the book...

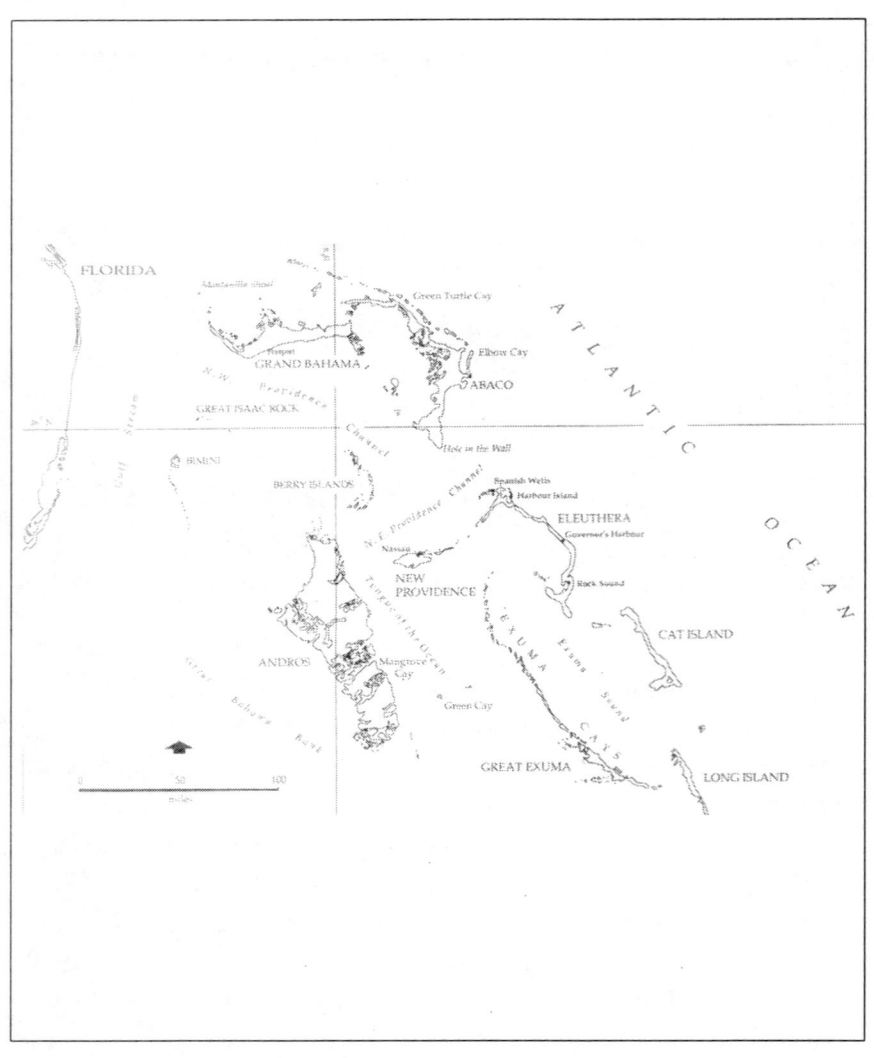

Map of the Northern Bahama Islands

It is perhaps always a good idea to look at the big picture first. Have you ever noticed on a map that the Bahamas look like a convoy of warships ominously sailing north... poised to attack the North American mainland? And one island—Grand Bahama—looks as if it is actually turning westward as if to launch an attack....!

Geographically Grand Bahama is interesting in another way too. All of the major islands of the Bahamas lie on the eastern side of a great Bank. (New Providence in a geographical sense is not 'major' and Inagua is a special case). Only Grand Bahama sits at the southern side of a Bank (the Little Bahama Bank).

Fundamental to our story is the limestone bedrock of the island that has been in place for millions of years...it has a long and interesting story to tell. It is 3 kilometres and more thick, in fairly pure form and, apart from crystalline formations, there is nothing else. No gold, no diamonds, no silver, nothing...

The limestone was chemically produced in the sea and supplemented by coral detritus to form the bedrock of the banks and the island. Internally the island is like Swiss cheese and has produced a fantastic underground cave system—among the longest in the world. The holes in the limerock contain a giant fresh water aquifer. Offshore to the south there is a magnificent fringing coral reef. To the north there is no clear line between land and sea that, throughout time has given map makers a great deal of trouble.

The limestone supports vegetation which in many ways is unique having evolved from Cuban and Antillean (not North American) origins. There are, for instance, 250 species of plants in the Lucayan National Park alone, supported in part on topsoil that scientists would have us believe, blew here from the Sahara!

Land based fauna includes the raccoon at the top of the food chain (an import from the 1930's), then we have several terrestrial small rodents (also imports), bats, birds, the interesting and unique curly tailed lizard, amphibians, snakes and insects a-plenty.

But it is the sea which is perhaps the most interesting and certainly the most prolific. The sea has animals that do not move and look like plants (sea fans), others build themselves into the shape of trees (or antlers if you prefer), then there are male sea creatures that produce offspring (sea horses), fish that change their sex (like groupers) and others that sting and bite (I do not need to tell you which they are). And a mollusc, the queen conch, that is an important staple of the Bahamian diet. In my research I noticed in an English dictionary published in the nineteenth century that a second definition of 'conch' was 'the white inhabitants of the Bahama Islands...'

Our human history can be traced to between 20,000 to 40,000 years ago with the migration of Asians to the Americas—via the Bering Strait. But only around the time of Christ did the Asian immigrants (by now native Americans) arrive in the Bahamas.

Interestingly the Bahama Islands were probably the very last territory discovered by the Native Americans in the Americas and Grand Bahama was very probably the very last island in the Bahamas and thus the Americas colonized by humankind!

Then, paradoxically, the Bahamas was the first country of the Americas to be discovered by Europeans. As the jingle goes:
In 1492 Columbus sailed the ocean blue...

Lucayan Indians—a painting by Bahamian artist Alton Lowe.

Early in the Christian Era immigrants from Hispaniola and Cuba had moved northwards up the chain of Bahamian islands. Originally, of the Siboney and Taino cultures, they adapted to life in the islands and developed an entirely new culture...they called themselves *Lukku Cairii*, we call them Lucayans.

Originally it was thought that most of the Lucayans were concentrated in the central Bahamas—now we know better. At Deadmans Reef for instance, a beach site has produced a prodigious number of artifacts...over 2000 at last count. It is perhaps the most productive archaeological site in the entire Bahamas!

Other sites have been found at many places along the south shore particularly at the Lucayan National Park and in Bahamia. The banks of Hawksbill Creek undoubtedly had Lucayan habitation sites but these unfortunately have been lost through development. Graveyards in the whiteland ecological zone just behind the beach often turn up Lucayan pottery shards. Since there was a tradition of travelling ever northward, when the Indians reached Grand Bahama they had nowhere else to go...and this just may account for why sites in Grand Bahama were so prolific.

The human story is recorded in two parts: prehistoric and historic. 'Prehistoric' is generally considered the time before history was written down. 'Historic' is of course the period from which we have written records.

And so the start of historic records for Grand Bahama commences in 1513. That was the year Ponce de Leon on his famous voyage looking for the *Fountain of Youth* found *la Vieja* (an old woman) on a cay near West End. It was significant: his encounter bridged the historic/pre-historic gap between the two worlds. The old Lucayan woman was one of the last of more than the estimated 40,000 Lucayans who lived in the Bahamas and had been either decimated by disease or carried off by the Spanish as slaves.

Ponce left two men to look for the *Fountain of Youth* in the northern Bahamas. They doubtless explored Grand Bahama and Bimini and then returned to Puerto Rico. Once there, the men claimed they had found the *Fountain of Youth* but their haggard and gaunt appearance clearly did not bear out their words! Needless to say no further expeditions were mounted to find the illusive fountain!

And so the islands were uninhabited for the next 135 years until the Eleutheran Adventurers arrived from Bermuda

Grand Bahama was doubtless visited by the Eleutherans and their descendants. It is even possible that some of the dyewood (Braziletto) that was sent to Harvard College in 1650 might have come from Grand Bahama. The dyewood was the biggest 'outside grant' to Harvard in its formative years....

Then there is another gap in our knowledge about the island. Governors came and went reporting to England that Grand Bahama was 'uninhabited as yet'. Well, it might not have had a permanent population but it was surely not overlooked by pirates... Uninhabited islands near important sea lanes were ideal places for pirates to lie in wait for unsuspecting shipping. One major shipwreck was found opposite to Taino Beach and the pirate involved was Dutchman Piet Heyn, whose deed was commemorated on a Cuban silver coin.

Why was Grand Bahama not settled? The main reason was probably its lack of natural harbours. Everything that Grand Bahama offered: lumber, fishing, land for agriculture and so on, was afforded by Andros which was much closer to Nassau—the capital and centre of commerce of the colony.

Then in 1792 the records show that there was a sale of 240 acres of land near the western end of the island. By 1806 we have evidence that one Joseph Smith had a plantation at West End and by 1836 there was a recorded population of 370 on the island. Interesting reports from commissioners from here onwards talk of the 'boisterous sea along the south coast', 'injurious burning of the land', 'declined in importance...' In these early days people had already started emigrating away from the island....

A few things happened in these years which just might have been witnessed by the people resident on Grand Bahama. In 1829 *HMS Monkey* intercepted *Midas* a Spanish slaving vessel en route from Af-

Suggestion for a monument to commemorate the Lucayan Indian occupation of a beachfront site at Deadmans Reef western Grand Bahama

rica to Havana. The two-masted schooner *Monkey* interestingly had been built in Jamaica. *Midas* tried to escape but she fired upon by *Monkey* and then boarded. Strangely the slaves were not freed in the Bahamas (possibly because there was almost nothing on the island to support them) but were taken to Cuba where it is to be hoped they were set free.

Grand Bahama undoubtedly featured in the story of wrecking. The names Fortune Point, Silver Point, Gold Rock may all be trying to tell us something! For good measure a famous American Roman Catholic bishop was wrecked on the island late in the 19th century.

Land grants give us a small insight into the patterns of habitation on the island. West End has been mentioned, both sides of Hawksbill Creek were inhabited. There was a sugar mill at Smiths Point. Petersons Cay had a small village and a Baptist Church (built in 1901).

(Old) Freetown was very likely named for slaves freed from slaving vessels that had been intercepted by the Royal Navy. Late in the nineteenth century people from Freetown used to walk to near Water Cay to catch the sponging vessels working the Little Bahama Bank. Not so long ago the path they used was still visible. And Water Cay once grew sisal in quantity and also produced many sponge fishermen. The persistent story about Greybeard the pirate using the cay cannot be corroborated however.

Gold Rock was once the administrative centre of the island, named in the early days, Golden Grove. High Rock was an early settlement with agriculture on the 'white land' with good fishing offshore. The same was true of Pelican Point. McLeans Town and Sweetings Cay came to prominence because of sponging with their easy access to the Little Bahama Bank. Drawbacks here were the paucity of fresh water and agricultural land.

I had the privilege of talking to the Rev Thomas Hield (born in1862) before he died. A centenarian who died at the age of 105 the good reverend gentleman used to walk the length of Grand Bahama every two weeks as a supervisor of the Baptist Church. He was a mine of information on the communities of the island.

At the turn of the century large scale lumbering became an important economic activity on the island. Turpentine was produced as a by-product of tree harvesting. Lumber was exported to Cuba and later was used as pit props in Britain and Germany. The lumber industry was, at this time, the largest employer in the private sector in the entire country.

...40 years later one lumberman was to put the island on the map of the world.

In the early 20th century not much happened on the island. To illustrate this fact the Commissioner reported that the revenue of the island was only £15. 5. 3! (Even at today's prices that is still less $300!) He claimed the morals of the islanders had improved (!) but, apart from John Martin, who owned 60 cows, and sponge fishing on the Bank there was little enterprise to be found in Grand Bahama. Indeed the island was loosing population once again!

All this was to change in 1919 when the United States passed the Volstead Prohibition Act. Seen from the viewpoint of today it was a remarkable idea. At the stroke of a pen it was thought that a whole nation would overnight stop drinking alcohol! Well it didn't work... and Nassau, Bimini and West End helped to frustrate the intent of the Act.

The most remarkable event at West End during Prohibition was the night one of the American-based 'mobs' raided the place. Armed with tommy guns they broke into liquor warehouses looking for cash. On this occasion Cecil Hepburn's father (see the note on Cecil later) was tied to a table while they ransacked his place looking for money. But there were lean pickings; the mobsters got perhaps $8000 in cash. Their raid was ill-starred however, since on the very same morning, the Nassau liquor merchants had sent their money (all $250,000 of it!) to Nassau on the leaky old mail boat! To keep law and order West End in these days had a commissioner and two unarmed policemen.

An aerial view of West End taken during Prohibition. Note the slips for the rum runner boats.

After Prohibition ended some developers came to Grand Bahama looking to build a city roughly located where Freeport is today. They prepared a map on which the site of their city was marked, it was to be called: Fairfield. But nothing more was heard of the venture.

In 1939 the population was just over 2000 people. It was not until well into the 1940's that the population of Grand Bahama exceeded that of the Lucayan Indians.

During WWII the Duke of Windsor (governor of the Bahamas at the time) visited the Grand Bahama Packing Company, later known as Bahama Seafoods. He arrived on the *Southern Cross* a yacht owned by Axel Wenner-Gren who was commonly believed to be Hitler's chief spy in the Bahamas.

In 1944 the Abaco Lumber Company moved to Grand Bahama. This was not so significant as the man who owned the company. That man was, of course, Wallace Groves.

The lumber company had a railway which ran on a permanent track between the harbour and Pine Ridge. The track ran along what we today call Government Road. It used to stop to take on water near what

>
>
> ### BAHAMIAN GEOGRAPHY
>
> The map shows our islands shaped like vessels a hundred miles off Florida's shoreline nestled ready, perhaps, to strike at a northern foe?
>
> No!
> The giant convoy is on the ocean floor rooted so silly talk of a hostile war fleet is refuted…
>
>

is today the Petroleum Products service station. More track was laid and then taken up as the lumbering operations expanded eastwards. Up until recently wooden sleepers (ties) could be seen at the edge of the road.

The company had two antediluvian steam locomotives numbers 4 and 5. One day Locomotive No. 5 exploded with the sound of a thunderbolt and killed and injured a few people. A government enquiry was instituted which found the cause to be human error. The locomotive engineer had closed the safety valve to increase steam pressure to climb a small incline…..then gone for lunch!

Just after the WWII Wallace Groves used to sit at the pink house at the slip at the mouth of Hawksbill Creek (the house was still there last time I looked). He dreamed that one day there would be a magnificent harbour where then, there were only mud flats, he dreamed of an international airport, he dreamed of schools, houses, churches in fact he dreamed of creating a major city.

And, as you all know, it all became a reality.

In 1955 on 5th August (I strongly believe this day should be declared a community holiday!) the Hawksbill Creek Agreement was signed between the government of the Bahamas and Wallace Groves.

And I will close here since the rest of the Grand Bahama story is well within living memory.

Hawksbill Creek Agreement signing. Standing: A G Knox-Johnson, L A W Orr, Sir Stafford Sands, Warren Levarity, Sir Robert Stapleton and Wallace Groves.

Hawksbill Creek Agreement

This is a note about the Hawksbill Creek Agreement, the legislation that brought Freeport into being. For a more thorough dissertation on this subject the reader may wish to refer to a talk Attorney Fred Smith gave in Freeport in 2004 (recorded in the archives of the *Freeport News*) and the video of a talk on the same subject given by Attorney Carey Leonard to the Rotary Club in Freeport in August 2010).

The Hawksbill Creek Agreement has been likened to the charters granted to the East India and Hudson's Bay companies. And, though on a smaller scale, there are real similarities, though in some respects, the 'owners' of Freeport enjoy even greater privileges than the nabobs of the imperial era. Since the 1970's Freeport has been a private company and is thus not answerable to shareholders or even governmental scrutiny and thus it provides no financial information on the Port-controlled companies to anybody. The Port Group of companies that collectively own and administer Freeport derive income from the sale of land, leases, service charges, licenses an other fees, in addition they collect revenue from the water supply monopoly and 50% of all revenue collected for the supply of electrical power to the entire island. Revenue is also derived from partial interests in other major companies such as Bahamas Shipyards, the Harbour Company and the waste management company. In short to be in control of the Port Authority is analogous to being the mayor of a small town who owns all the land, the utility companies, and all the tax revenue—and not having to declare how much money is harvested or how it is spent. With only two titled British families now controlling the Port Group of companies commentators have suggested that Freeport (in 2009) in many respects resembles a fiefdom.

Supplemental Agreement

After the Hawksbill Creek Agreement another milestone was passed in 1960 with promulgation of the Supplemental Agreement. The following is an extract from the book 'Grand Bahama' that explains the agreement which allowed the Port Authority to promote tourism and real estate in the Port Area. It also added the word 'Lucaya' to our lexicon.

As 1955 saw the birth of the Freeport venture so 11 July, 1960 witnessed its coming of age. Largely due to the influence of Sir Stafford Sands, the original Hawksbill Creek Agreement was enhanced by a further agreement, known as the Supplemental Agreement that was signed by the Government and the Port Authority. This Agreement acknowledged the accomplishments of the Port Authority by confirming that the Port Authority had dredged the harbour channels, constructed a bunkering base and wharf and complied with all the other obligations of the Principal Agreement. It further granted to the Port Authority additional acreage of land at a nominal price north of the original 50,000 acres extending between Seagrape and Gold Rock Creek. In consideration of this it was mutually agreed that the original Hawksbill Creek Agreement would be amended by requiring the Port Authority to build a 200-room luxury hotel by the 31st December 1963, and to provide free education for school children living within the Port area; it also reaffirmed that the Port Authority was to continue to promote and encourage the establishment of lawful business enterprises in Freeport and (in clause 4) it makes an interesting reference to the possible establishment of future municipal government by way of a 'local authority'.

This Supplemental Agreement was the touchstone for the development of Freeport as a bona fide city. Without it Freeport would have been a not very pretty industrial hub huddled around the deepwater harbour.

The Queen Visits

In 1967 HM Queen Elizabeth II visited Nassau. Wallace Groves asked me to design the exhibition stand for Freeport and invited my wife and I to be in his party to be presented to the Queen (Sir Charles Hayward was the other member). Incidentally my wife Isabelle is also an architect with exhibition design experience from Canada. She designed the Grand Bahama Island exhibit.

The Freeport exhibit had many photos of Freeport and a rotating

New Court House in Freeport opened by HM Queen Elizabeth II in 1994

display of a conglomerate of silver coins found recently in a wreck from Grand Bahama (worth about $50,000 at the time). The Duke of Edinburgh asked, half jokingly, if the Crown, citing ancient statutes, could not lay claim to at least 50% of the coins.

The whole exhibit was called *Bahamarama* and was a showcase for all the inhabited islands of the archipelago. It was designed by the doyen of architectural profession at the time, Ray Nathaniels. (Interestingly I took Ray's architectural position in Tripoli, Libya after he left. I only met him for the first time four years later when I came to the Bahamas. Incidentally, I heard on the news today some of the radio and telecommunications buildings I designed in Libya had probably been destroyed in the recent revolt—20/2/11).

The Queen visited the Bahamas again and this time came to Freeport in 1994 where she opened the magnificent new Court House on The Mall. She heaped praise on Sir Jack and Edward St George for constructing the edifice but then also lauded them as 'the creators of Freeport' omitting to mention that there was somebody else who had a lot to do with its creation and development.

Martin Dale and Prince Rainier of Monaco

Martin A Dale joined the Port Authority in 1965 as a vice-president (he claimed the additional title of 'Adviser to the President' which I remember did not go down too well with the other vice-presidents). Dale had previously been economic advisor to Prince Rainier of Monaco. While in the Principality, Charles de Gaulle, then the President of France, let it be known he was not happy with the choice of an American *wunderkinder* in what was and is (arguably) a virtual province of France. The American wife of Rainier, Grace Kelly probably suggested the appointment. Martin's wife Joan, who was a Grace Kelly look-alike, sometimes stood in for Princess Grace for minor events or when security was likely to be a problem.

Groves, through Martin Dale, invited Prince Rainier to visit Freeport since the Prince claimed to be intrigued by a casino in the Lucayan Beach Hotel that was named the 'Monte Carlo Room'. He visited the casino of course and also the International Bazaar where he visited the Mexican boutique: 'Azteca de Oro'. He remarked on the colourful displays and admired some abalone bottle openers—that were given to him as a souvenir of his visit.

Dale lasted only about two years in Freeport then left to work with Revlon in New York with the same two corporate titles.

Gambling Commission

Late in 1967 a Commission on Gambling held court in Freeport and Nassau. The terms of reference of the Commission required them to take a close look at:

- whether members of the Government had received pecuniary benefit from the introduction or operation of the casinos;
- the suitability of persons employed in the casino;
- the legislation and administration regarding casino gambling;
- the accounting, calculating and distribution of profits of the casinos and the recipients thereof; and
- any recipients of payments not disclosed in the accounts.

The Commission of Enquiry was able to air a lot of dirty washing in discovering irregularities, exposing undesirables and unraveling primitive and abstruse bookkeeping. It was patently clear that no one knew how much money Bahamas Amusements made at its casino at the Lucayan Beach Hotel, nor exactly who had received a 'cut'. The Commission expressed considerable concern 'that the consultants (members of the UBP Government) who were members of the Council should ever have allowed themselves to be put in the position where a conflict

Lucayan Beach Hotel and the partly dredged Bell Channel Bay in 1963.

of interest would surely have arisen'. The Commission suggested that gambling in the Bahamas be the subject of a Gaming Act supervised by a non-partisan Commission on Gambling; that citizens of the United States should not be employed in any capacity directly involved with the gambling operation; and the that adult Bahamians be permitted to play at the casinos. The recommendation concerning the employment of American citizens was later conveniently forgotten but allowing Bahamians to gamble was followed.

The Government Commission of Enquiry also brought to light the fact that many members of the Executive Council had been lobbied and offered consultancy fees that were clearly similar to bribes. Sir Roland Symonette, was very disturbed. Soon to become the first Premier of The Bahamas, with the passage of a new constitution in 1964, Sir Roland was morally opposed to gambling. And, even though he finally accepted a modest consultancy arrangement with DEVCO, he still could not bring himself to vote for the Certificate of Exemption. Shortly after this difficult and morally ambiguous period, Symonette became Premier and resigned his consultancy, having collected only £5,000 as a consultancy fee. The Bahamas was learning the maxim about gambling that Casinos are always in a constant struggle to either keep racketeers out and/or to convince gaming authorities they are clean. The Monte Carlo Casino now found itself plumb in the middle of this dilemma.

Wallace Groves

I may be one of the few people left who knew Wallace Groves personally. He was not an easy person to know. For somebody as important as he became in Bahamian history he was exceedingly reticent. But let's start at the beginning. He was a tunnel-visioned genius. He graduated at Georgetown University with three degrees all obtained in the same year—it had never been done before and, as far as I know, it is something that has not been done since. He became a Wall Street high flyer. He lived a millionaire life-style and married an attractive Hollywood starlet. Then it happened. In the anti-profiteering milieu of the WWII he was convicted of financial crimes and sent to prison. To him it was like the end of the world. His wife divorced him, many of his high-flying friends deserted him, Wall Street was closed to him.

The Oakes affair was still fresh in everybody's memory at this time and so perhaps it was this that made him conscious of the Bahamas. Anyway, whatever the reason, he moved to the islands and bought the ailing Abaco Lumber Company and settled into an idyllic private world at Little Whale Cay in the Berry Islands. For about ten years the company was engaged in lumbering in Grand Bahama and it was here that he had a dream of developing a new community around the old lumber slip at the mouth of Hawksbill Creek. With the help of a friendly Bay Street-dominated government, the Hawksbill Creek Agreement offering exceptional concessions, came into being. I cover much of the history of the meteoric growth of Freeport from its inception in my book 'Grand Bahama'.

But what about the man himself?

Well, first Groves had an iron will to succeed. He had a prodigious memory. He had a great understanding of all the aspects of devel-

The following poem was written to commemorate Founders Day, August 5th. Hopefully one day the date will receive recognition as a public holiday.

ODE TO THE FREEPORT FOUNDER

On the nation's northern flank
near the Little Bahama Bank,
unblessed by nature's largess
was an isle, flat and harbour-less.
But then in year nineteen fifty five
Grand Bahama was to spring alive
because the Hawksbill Creek accord
parlayed by a new Proprietor Lord
became manifest from a grand decision
and Wallace Groves' grit and vision.
'new city, bah!' said some with derision.
But the bold concept forgotten by time
will perhaps be recalled by this rhyme.

oping a new community and he was able to use people to his advantage. He was able to get DK Ludwig to build the deepwater harbour for virtually nothing, then he got Big Lou Chesler to finance the Grand Bahama Development Company that in turn built the Lucayan Beach Hotel, a marina and canals, greatly extended the road system, introduced large scale retail land sales and most importantly, established a major casino on the island. It was Faustian pact however.

Groves knew his partner well, he said many times his relationship with Chesler was like 'oil and water'. But the liaison was immensely important to the development of the island. However, when the full picture of the casino and its operation became public he cut his ties with Chesler. I was outside the board room the day the split occurred and will never forget the look on Chesler's face as he stormed out of the office. But Chesler had actually done quite well out of Freeport and he took some of the funds to develop a small community on

The Groves Mausoleum on Sunrise Highway, Freeport.

Great Harbour Cay. But he did not have Groves' vision and know-how and neglected to solve the problem of easy and affordable access to the island.

After this everything continued to go well for Groves, perhaps too well, that is until the majority rule government took over in the Bahamas. Then the expatriate character of Freeport was seriously questioned and Groves' Bay Street associates were reviled and the irregularities in gambling on the island were highlighted. The new government was determined to take Freeport on a new course even if, in the words of the new prime minister, it had to 'break'

By three ways is wisdom best expressed:
First, by reflection, which is the noblest;
Second, by imitation, which is the easiest;
and third by experience, which is the bitterest.

Confucius

Freeport. And break it did. When Groves reached his 70th birthday he perhaps made the second greatest mistake of his life by selling out to Jack (later Sir Jack) Hayward and Edward St George (the latter of whom had a minor interest initially) at a figure that probably undervalued Groves' investment. Indeed once the sale was completed Groves tried to purchase back part of the real estate but it was too late. The die was cast. A few years thereafter he had a heart attack and a short time later he passed away. He is interred with his wife Georgette in a mausoleum adjacent to Mary Star of the Sea Church on Sunrise Highway in Freeport.

But the saddest thing of all is that so few people today appreciate the fantastic achievement he wrought in creating the Second City in the Bahamas.

Above: Aerial photograph of the Lucayan Beach subdivision showing building work on the Groves and Hayward houses near the beach. The site of the future Holiday Inn is to the right of the subdivision. The Gonsalves house is on Hawaii Avenue centre left.
Below: Aerial photograph of the Lucayan 'strip' as it is today.

News Release—Development Company Stock Sale

Wallace Groves, President of the Grand Bahama Port Authority, and Louis Chesler, a large stockholder in the Grand Bahama Development Company, in which the Port Authority is majority owner, announced jointly the termination of Mr. Chesler's connections with the Development Company.

Mr. Chesler has sold the Port Authority 200,000 shares of his Development Company shares at a price substantially in excess of his purchase costs in 1960, when he was a founder of the Development Company, which has been responsible for much of the residential, land and hotel development of this fast-growing Island.

He has placed his remaining shares in escrow on a short-term option to the Port Authority.

In addition, Mr. Chesler has arranged a mutually satisfactory termination of his sales contract with the Development Company.

In commenting on Mr. Chesler's ending of a five-year relationship on Grand Bahama Island, Mr. Groves paid tribute to him. He said, "There is no question that Mr. Chesler's remarkable gifts of salesmanship, his vision and his drive have contributed most significantly to the great advance of this Island. Inasmuch as Mr. Chesler has now severed all his business connections on the Island, he has said that he intends to move from Grand Bahama but that he will always have warm feelings for the residents of the island and for the success of the Development Company. He further stated that he holds in high regard the officers of both the Development Company and the Port Authority." ■

This was almost certainly written by Carl Livingston who was a full time PR man on the staff of the Port Authority/Devco at the time. It's interesting how News Releases sometimes gloss over the real facts.

D. K. Ludwig Returns

After a nearly ten year hiatus DK Ludwig returned to Freeport in 1965 with plans to build hotels and two golf course subdivisions. I met him in Groves' office to discuss the land he was to acquire near the centre of Freeport. It was actually located at the southwest quadrant of Sunrise Highway and The Mall crossroads. He was intrigued by the local name for a four way intersection so he chose the name 'Crossroads' for his company that was later to develop Bahamia and the Kings Inn/Princess Properties (later taken over by Harcourt) and the International Bazaar.

We discussed the type of architecture that would be most appropriate for the hotel. I suggested it should be modern but follow the 'aesthetically' appropriate style of traditional Bahamian architecture. He jumped at word 'aesthetically' and said, 'never use that word in my presence young man—aesthetics cost money!'

I later understood that he had been badly burned in Mexico City where he had spent over a million dollars on a building on the main thoroughfare, Paseo de la Reforma. One day he decided he should visit the city to take a look at the progress. When he arrived in Mexico he discovered a big hole in the ground with foundations in evidence but not much else. He stopped work immediately and walked away from the project.

D. K. Ludwig

D K Ludwig at the time reputed to be one of the richest men in the world.

Lynden O. Pindling Comes to Town

In late 1966 the Port Authority received a request from the fledgling Progressive Liberal Party (PLP) for the use of the Freeport supermarket parking lot for a political rally. The speaker was a young Lynden O Pindling the leader of the Opposition in the House of Assembly. For reasons I do not recall I was chosen to coordinate the event which merely meant getting a podium installed and arranging an electrical connection for the lights.

I arrived in the evening a short while before Mr Pindling arrived to confirm that the podium was in place and a lighting connection was available. Meanwhile an enormous crowd (by the standards of the day) was assembling. I was just about to leave when LOP arrived and beckoned to me before mounting the podium. I suppose I must have been conspicuous because I was the only person present with a pale complexion. He inquired as to who I was and asked me to take a seat next to him on the podium. I could hardly refuse an important visiting politician so there I sat down trying to look at ease facing a multitude of people who, for all I knew, might turn boisterous.

Pindling's speech was captivating. There was little talk about an enlightened social and economic programme for the Bahamas but lots of innuendo, parables almost, and quotations from the Bible, including several references to the opening of the Red Sea than invoked numerous cries of 'Moses come!' The future prime minister certainly knew how to galvanise a crowd. I remember too he spoke with a stronger dialect than in later years and raised the biggest applause when he digressed into a little story about a gum elemi tree that everybody—except me—understood.

Sir Lynden Pindling

Sir Lynden Pindling and his party went on to rule the Bahamas for 25 long years. He and his party did great work during the first two 5-year terms but everyone knows the noble Lord's statement about absolute power. ...and yes, it did tend to corrupt. Pindling was a fine orator. Not of the first rank of course but right up there with some of the best orators.

Name Dropping

>
>
> GREAT ORATORS
>
> Two of the greatest statesmen of all time
> Were Lincoln and Churchill I surmise
> Their power was not in the politics they espoused
> But rather in the eloquence of the words they mouthed
>
>

A long list of luminaries have visited Freeport. Obviously all the big names on the Bahamian political scene have been to Freeport (particularly around election time). Governors too have visited, perhaps the most important of them was Lord Ranfurly (for whom a roundabout is named). He was a mentor to Wallace Groves and he also arranged for Groves to meet Sir Charles Hayward who dropped a million pounds Sterling into the Port Authority kitty.

The early years saw a lot of D. K. Ludwig reputedly America's richest man at the time. Bacardi came to invest but did not like the rawness of early Freeport so he built a distillery in Nassau instead. James Rand inventor and industrialist built the hospital and also gave his name to the Rand Nature Centre. An occasional guest of James Rand was Werner von Braun the rocket scientist. Kemmons Wilson the founder of Holiday Inn appropriately enough built a Holiday Inn (now called the Breakers). Mark Johnson a champion ocean racer lived in Freeport for a time. Besides winning several international trophies he actually built a world class yacht in Freeport, the *Windward Passage* (and his Dad built the Charthouse restaurant on Sunrise Highway).

For the consecration of Mary Star of Sea church (the name was selected by Groves incidentally) about six bishops visited, at least one abbot and the Dean of Georgetown University (Groves later gave his old university a large endowment later). Freeport has welcomed royalty and nobility, QEII visited to open the Court House, Queen Quet

Big 'Lou' Chesler, a Hollywood starlet and her husband, Mrs Chesler and Rick Ricardo.

of the Gullah Geechee Nation visited and Prince Hohenlohe came with a view to investing—but didn't, likewise Shaun Alexander the son of Lord Alexander of Tunis, Count Nostiz of Austria, and Canadian mogul Alexis Nihon. The Spanish Duchess of Marchena came often but used a name like 'Mrs Howard' to avoid attention. The Duke of Grafton (Lady Henrietta St Georges' father) stayed as did his son, Lord Euston. Lord Denby and several other peers made an appearance as did Dame Maggie Thatcher. Many, many film stars visited, Joan Crawford being one of the first. She was followed by Yul Brunner, and many American TV personalities. Film stars also included Joan Collins (a snitch told me she had several massages while in Freeport), Peter O'Toole of Laurence of Arabia fame came and Tom Jones visited more than once and sang his heart out at the Casino. Count Basie (not a real Count of course) lived in Freeport but, as far I recall, never performed there.

John Travolta had a second home in West End. His son died there tragically a few years ago. Pierre Berton the Canadian media personality gave a talk at Rotary. And one star from the silent film era to make an appearance in the early 60's was Gilda Dahlberg (who was probably an ex-flame of Wallace Groves). Howard Hughes came to Freeport and checked into the Xanadu Hotel claiming he was not a guest. He was right. He had just bought the hotel and was living there in splendid

Howard Hughes

Howard Hughes who owned and resided at the Xanadu Hotel for a time.

isolation on the two top floors. Sir Freddie Laker ran an airline from Freeport and lived for a time just down the street from the Xanadu in Ocean Isle. Robert Mugabe of Zimbabwe came hoping to find a second home as a refuge, ditto OJ Simpson.

Pierre Trudeau prime minister of Canada visited one Sunday and complained he had difficulty finding downtown Freeport. Nelson Mandela came for a brief visit and didn't even bother to look. Robert Rubin with numerous financiers in his wake visited often, most were keen bone fishermen and sought privacy. It may say something about these financial mavens that they find sport in snaring small animals... The whole tribe of the Commonwealth Press Corps came to town once and conventions without number arrived with important keynote speakers. Kenneth Galbraith the economist, and Buckminster Fuller a renaissance man, both gave lectures on the island. Count Marigny the man acquitted after the murder of Sir Harry Oakes paid a brief visit to Freeport late in life. Marigny claimed he met a man on his visit who could have been a material witness in the case but disappeared during the trial.

Rex Nettleford the Jamaican impresario visited more than once, and talking about the performing arts, Freeport also played host to the Alvin Hailey dancers and the Miami Opera (now called the Florida Grand Opera). Lesser lights like Jimmy the Greek came and produced a promotional film for the island so did Olympian Michael Phelps. Justin Hill the well-known English writer and American pop singer whose stage name was Sebastian Bach were actually born in Freeport. The actors of 'Pirates of the Caribbean' also paid a brief call to Gold Rock Creek and left a big wet hole as a souvenir of their visit. Included in the cast were Keira Knightley, Orlando Bloom, Johnny Depp and

Geoffrey Rush (I was at the airport when Keira Knightley, was fingerprinted and photographed by US Immigration control prior to being permitted to enter the United States). She took it very well and joked that most people *paid* to take photographs of her.

The Mayor of Miami Beach came years before on an official visit with armed bodyguards who were unceremoniously disarmed by the Royal Bahamas Police.

And of course there were many more VIPs who came visiting but these are some that immediately come to mind.

The reference to Howard Hughes and Xanadu brings to mind the poet Coleridge and how he might have viewed the Freeport reference to Xanadu.

ORIGINAL COLERIDGE

In Xanadu did Kubla Khan
A stately pleasure dome decree
Where Alph the sacred river ran
Through caverns fathomless to man
Down to the sunlit sea

UPDATED COLERIDGE

Near Xanadu—as you will see
A domed casino was the decree
While deep below the
island ran
caverned rivers—mapped by man
that boil up in a sunlit sea

Abstruse is obscurantism seen at an angle.

Early Freeport Personalities

Sir Albert Miller

Recognized for his exceptional organizational abilities.

Groves was ably assisted by the redoubtable Keith Gonsalves who was attracted away from a senior position with Barclays Bank. Newly arrived from Nassau and having left the Royal Bahamas Police was Albert (later Sir Albert) Miller OSMG who initially did fine service with tourist promotion working his way up to be appointed as one of three Co-Chairmen of the Port and its associated companies. Sir Albert was recognized for his exceptional organizational abilities and was later made, while still with the Port Authority, chairman of BEC and Batelco two major Bahamian utilities.

The incorrigible Major Bernie Bernard was Corporate Secretary of the Port Authority in the early days and Ray Tower was the aggressive legal counsel who overstepped the bounds and challenged the new government's policy towards Freeport. He was soon on a plane back to Canada. Major Bernard left to take up a short-lived position in the South Seas a little later. George Kates was the dynamic president of the Grand Bahama Development Company for a time and under his wing Albert Grey rose to prominence in the company. Kates ended up living in Tehachapi in California.

Doug Silvera yo-yoed between Freeport Construction Company and the Port Authority doing sterling work for both companies. After Ray Tower left Michael Boyce took over the legal reins working for a short time with Willie Moss as legal counsel. After Sir Jack Hayward and Edward St George stepped into Wallace Groves' shoes their tenure at the Port Authority was even longer than that of Groves but for many reasons did not accomplish as much. Later Willie Moss was elevated to president of the Port Authority a position she later shared with Julian

Francis for a year. Since then several people have been appointed interim Chairmen of the Port Authority presumably marking time until a new owner appears.

The offices of the Grand Bahama Port Authority in Freeport. In 2005, to commemorate the first 50 years since the signing of the Hawksbill Creek Agreement, an exhibit was mounted in the Public Library opposite.

But don't take my word for it. Other writers have a very different perspective on Freeport. Here is an extract from someone who writes his insights from Massachusetts. His interesting website is: www.jabezcorner.com/Grand_Bahama/month2.htm

◆

What history there is has been ably covered by Peter Barratt in his Grand Bahama (Newton Abbott, Devon, 1972; second ed., London, 1982). But once Mr. Barratt's excellent work has been finished, there may be a lingering curiosity about some of the intriguing references that he cites. This page is intended to assuage that to some extent.

Searching for any Bahamian history on the Internet, let alone Grand Bahamian history, returns only brief and repetitive synopses which scarcely do justice to the subject. All of the wonderful work of Gail Saunders and Michael Craton has apparently made no impact on cyberspace. For this reason I prefer to leave the description of these wonders to such an authoritative publication as the Bahamas Handbook.

Physically Grand Bahama, with its flat dusty miles of pine woods, is like chunk of inland Florida chopped off and set afloat sixty miles offshore. Except for the closer presence of the sea you might as well be in the outskirts of Orlando or Ocala. Since much of the land development taking place on Grand Bahama is being done by the same American interests as are transforming the state of Florida into a single super-Levittown, the resemblance between the two grows daily more disquieting.

In addition to industrial development and home sites, Grand Bahama offers gambling. For twenty-four hours a day there is a busy shuttling back and forth between the mainland and the Miami-Beach-baroque corridors of the Lucayan Beach Hotel. Its gambling casino is a handsome thing of yellow damask walls and crystal chandeliers. To spend your winnings you have a choice of La Mer Lounge, the Club La Perruche, the Monaco Bar and several restaurants whose prices are scaled according to their gastronomic heights. When they first reported for duty on Grand Bahama the 'bunnies' of the Lucayan Beach Hotel were understandably bewildered by the frontier-town atmosphere of the town. They have since become adjusted, reconciled to such events as the expected arrival, on the day I was there, of a five-hundred-man convention of insurance salesmen from Missouri and Kansas...

In a recent poll conducted by the Nassau *Tribune* among visitors to Freeport, the chief conclusion was: 'Though sun and sea are an attraction, the general tourist reaction to Freeport was that of a frontier town lacking beauty, charm, good food, good service, good shopping or anything to do. The only redeeming factor was gambling'. The editorial reluctantly came to the conclusion that perhaps the Government should have some share in the profits of gambling, estimated at more than £7,000,000, 'a move which should substantially strengthen the financial future even if it does not improve the moral climate'.

And there were more insights identified by Jabez Corner. None of them very flattering. . .

Moral Panic in the '60s: Gambling and Grand Bahama

In the mid 1960s, the legalization of casino gambling in the Bahamas touched off fears among U.S. authorities that the dreaded Mafia—as personified by Meyer Lansky—might be having a field day in the islands. The excitement began in October 1966 with a Wall Street Journal article revealing conniving and corruption between Wallace Groves' Grand Bahama Development Co. and the old-guard Bahamian leadership starring the redoubtable Sir Stafford Sands and the Bay Street Boys. The following year Life magazine (Feb. 3, 1967) and the Saturday Evening Post (Feb. 25, 1967) joined in the fun. Ed Reid's chapter adds a little about Lou Chesler... Since much of this concerned Grand Bahama, I have included these articles, one from Newsweek (1964) and a part of an article from Queen, (25 Oct.,1967), as historical fodder for the interested reader.

The entrance to the Moorish-style El Casino (the dome has since been demolished).

- Davidson, Bill. The Mafia: Shadow of Evil on an Island in the Sun
- Karmin, Monroe W. and Penn, Stanley. Las Vegas East.
- Oulahan, Richard, and Lambert, William. The Scandal in the Bahamas
- Leslie, Ann. A Month in the Life of the Bahamas. (selection)
- Bonanaza in the Bahamas (1964)
- Reid, Ed. "Bahamas Hoodlum Sea" (chap. 7 from The Grim Reapers- 1970)

The brief bibliography above makes reference to some interesting sensationalist journalism but some of the quoted sources lack strict accuracy.

> If we do not learn from history
> We hand stupidity a victory

The Port Authority Goes Shopping

After the change of government it was clear to the Port Authority it would not be 'business as usual'. Groves had stepped down from being CEO and some American managers were brought in who acted as if they were still in Boise, Idaho. The Port by this time had become a public company merging with Benguet a gold mining company in the Philippines. The watchword was now 'diversification' and for a time, for me at least, it had a short term benefit. The new company now went shopping. I was sent on a mission with Doug Silvera to look at land in California for possible purchase. We went to see a parcel of land near Bakersfield sitting astride the St Andreas Fault. The land was promptly bought and Doug planned a golf course on top of the potential earthquake fault line! The development was soon a success and was sold at a profit. 'Time' magazine even featured it after it had changed hands.

Then with another Port Authority executive I was sent on other missions to seek potential land acquisitions. On these I went to Corpus Christi, Texas, Mexico City, Acapulco, Vancouver and Spain (where we met the sister of Franco who wanted us to purchase land in the Costa del Sol). And I was not the only person travelling overseas. Other executives went to Turkey and they later visited and actually purchased land in Fuertaventura in the Canary Islands. Again this project was a success but was quickly sold off. Another chunk of land was bought at Orlando that was immediately sold at profit to you-can-guess-who. All this diversification sent a message to the new government that the Port was not going to spend money in Freeport if the new government was going to be unfriendly.

Wallace Groves—A Postscript

As referred to above, I published 'Grand Bahama' in England and the United Sates simultaneously in 1972. It was a hard cover book with a jacket illustration of the Lucayan Beach Hotel and a very raw-looking view of Bell Channel Bay. It is a good feeling to see your name in print for the first time! I hand-delivered six copies of the book to Wallace Groves at his farm ('ranch' might be a better word) in Devon. Having just retired he purchased a magnificent manor house-type farm and assembled the largest herd of the breed of South Devon cattle in Britain—and probably the world. He also created an airstrip on his land. He and his wife Georgette sometimes took their private plane to go shopping in Zurich because they did not like the traffic in London! But they found life a bit quiet in Devon so they soon moved on to Don Mills near Toronto for a short time. Then they returned south and bought penthouse apartments first in Key Biscayne and then in Aventura in Miami. They still kept up the palatial house in Freeport and Groves took over Discovery House from the Development Company as his office. This was clearly a restless time in his life and, though he never mentioned it, he clearly missed being the virtual czar of Freeport. Sadly Georgette, his supportive wife of many years, died before him. Wallace died shortly afterwards in Florida. His death was quite unexpected, he had told us on more than one occasion that he expected to live a long life since his mother died at 98 on the way to a beauty parlour. Groves body was brought back to Freeport where he was buried next to his wife in a mausoleum I designed near to Mary Star of the Sea. One of his last requests was that as an epitaph the words *Stella Maris—Ora pro Nobis* (Mary Star of the Sea—Pray for Us) be engraved inside the mausoleum.

> ### A PORT AUTHORITY PROMISE
>
> The Grand Bahama Port Authority
> Issues a solemn solid warranty
> And the promise of no taxes! Snakes alive!
> Well, that's only until twenty fifty five…

ENVIRONMENT

This is a terrible commentary on over-fishing and the state of coral reefs throughout the Bahamas and the world.

The Vanishing Reef

In the mid-1960's there was a sailing boat named the 'Big Jimbo' that every day took visitors fishing on the continuous fringing reef just off Lucayan Beach. Sometimes there were as many as 40 people aboard, all with boat-supplied fishing rods. Almost everybody caught something, some people several fish: Queen Triggers, groupers, snappers, grunts and even moray eels. Nowadays you will be lucky if you catch a fish in this location in an hour or more. And the reef? Now totally vanished except for an over-visited portion of the original reef near the Bahama Reef entrance canal.

And the reason for the destroyed coral reefs?

Overfishing, pollution, global warming, disease, turbidity caused by groynes and canals. Nobody seems to know the exact cause.

LETTER TO THE EDITOR:

WANTED—A BAHAMIAN WANGARI MAATHAI

When Wangari Maathai, the first African female recipient of the Nobel Peace prize, accepted the honour, she said she hoped the world would follow her example in trying to save the natural environment. Maathai is particularly concerned in preserving world forests. Yet in the Bahamas, we destroy trees (whether in a forest or not) for buildings and a variety of other uses at an alarming rate. There is seldom any selective cutting, the 'male' bulldozer operator (remember men are from Mars) usually ploughs through the land until hardly a blade of grass is left. What is needed are women (from Venus, Fox Hill and/or Martin Town) who care enough to nurture our environment, rein in the wanton destruction of trees and, at the same time, start a tree-planting programme that will offset the waste of this precious resource. If this happens Maathai's message will have been heard in our one small corner of the globe at least.

Peter Barratt

(The letter above was written after Wangari Maathai was awarded the Nobel Prize. It was published in the local newspaper.)

I am afraid the letter had not the slightest effect on the natural environment at the time. It was followed up by a poem that pays homage to the often forgotten pine trees.

ODE TO THE GRAND BAHAMIAN PINE

A mantle of straight and lofty pine
a forest seventy miles in line.
Grand Bahama, a stately forest boasts
stretching wide from both its coasts,
that, in times past, was partly lumbered
providing pit props and logs un-numbered.
But most important, it was the source
of funds to create, the 'Free-Port'.

Bahamian straight and lofty pines,
the raison d'etre of Freeport.

> **EXTINCTION IS FOREVER**
>
> For all creatures small, large and in between
> rare forms of life extinguished and unseen
> their record of existence sadly wiped clean
> perished now as though they had never been.

I am probably alone in drawing attention to the undesirable clearing of public land adjacent to arterial roads from lots that already gain access from an interior service road. The result is a hodgepodge of chain link fences mis-matched walls and, worst of all, illegal access onto arterial roads. It is dangerous and unsightly but no action is ever taken. Then there is the indiscriminate clearing of building lots where natural vegetation could have been retained. Here's a letter that was published on the subject (next page).

Predictably, to date no action has been taken, though the Environmental Department of the government recently (2010) held a poorly attended seminar in Freeport about the necessity to preserve the pine forest. We will have to wait to see if anything changes.

> **MOTIVE FORCE OF THE LEVIATHON**
>
> Consider the bulk of the prodigious
> humpbacked whale
> That has such mighty power in its fluke (or tail)
> In the natural world it has the greatest
> source of motion
> In the entire animal kingdom—on the earth
> or in the ocean

LETTER TO THE EDITOR:

5 August 2004

DESCRATION OF THE PINELAND

It seems that no action has yet been taken to stop the wholesale removal of pine trees on building sites. Clearly some trees and other vegetation must be removed for building operations but it makes no sense to bulldoze down every single tree on the lot. And anyway, it is against the law!

Polite observations decrying the practice have got nowhere even though the Caribbean pine tree is one of only ten trees on the declaration of Protected Trees Order in The Bahamas Government Conservation and Protection of the Physical Landscape Act 1997. Recently an environmental report suggested that in the Freeport Area the removal of trees is regulated through building permits issued by the Grand Bahama Development Company (a GBPA Group company) in accordance with the Hawksbill Creek Agreement. Clearly the Order is not being followed.

If the Port Authority will not police the unnecessary removal of pine trees (and other significant native vegetation) perhaps the pertinent Department of the Bahamas Government should step in and see that the law is followed.

CATHARTES AURA

Did you know that scrawny road-kill black bird
is a vulture/turkey buzzard/John or carrion crow
there's a Latin name too—that's a six word bird!
...but there's more you need to know

It can be compared with eagles when in flight
its soaring aerial pirouettes are a sheer delight
but its face is devoid of avian beauty though
...anything else you need to know?

A wing span of about two hundred centimetres
a purplish/red head and neck are among its features
but the bird does not sing, chirp, call or cackle, so...
there's not much else you need to know

Indeed it is without vocal chords called syrinxes
so the bird 's only expletives are grunts and hisses
and no surprise....it counts man as its only foe
now, surely there's nothing more you need to know!

Turkey buzzards are rare sight in New Providence but in Freeport there always seems to be a few flying aerial surveillance missions over Grand Bahama. They can also frequently be seen eating the remains of dead animals and KFC debris on the beaches and roads.

> Question: What should you do if you see an endangered animal eating endangered plants?

We are finding out more about pre-history on the island. Marine archaeologists have found evidence of crocodiles and there were doubtless other monsters on the island from the era of the dinosaurs. There has long been a legend about a bird-like animal that stalked the woods of Andros. Some scientists suggest the folklore about the animal might have some basis in fact. Since with few predators a flightless bird, like an emu or ostrich, might have existed on the island in the distant past. And, it follows, that if it lived in an extensive pine forest in Andros then why not in other pineland islands like Grand Bahama? Here is how poetess Telcine Turner explained the animal, locally called a 'chick charney', in verse.

> ### A STRAGE DICHOTOMY
>
> Of all the animals upon the earth
> just one understands, at birth,
> it is naked ... just think about it !
> His strange attire, a really close fit
> that he exchanges through time
> just like garments on human kind.
> And what may that animal be?
> Why, the lowly hermit crab is he!

He had a queer and mixed up form
Like none I'd ever seen.
His arms were bird, his ears were mouse
His legs were in between.

> **If a hermit crab doesn't find a shell**
> **is it naked or homeless?**

Lucayan National Park

In the 1980's I had just obtained a flying license and often flew along southern coast of Grand Bahama. From the air I followed the course of Gold Rock Creek and could see that, besides the Creek there was an exceptionally fine beach, an offshore 'rock' (Gold Rock) and inland there was a hammock area that I knew contained many caves. At 1000 feet in the air I had the idea of creating a National Park in this area. I took my idea to the Grand Development Company and at first I did not get anywhere but then Sir Jack Hayward piped up to say that he had travelled down the Creek by boat and he thought it was one of the most spectacular inland sights he had seen in the Bahamas. That clinched it! We drew a boundary around the most significant areas that came to about forty acres. Well that looked good on paper but suddenly events overtook the idea. John Hinchcliffe the Harbour Master at the time was looking for a project for Operation Raleigh a youth venture group sponsored by the Prince of Wales. Bingo! Suddenly we had dozens of

The old bridge over Gold Rock Creek constructed by David Knowles and the Venturers of Operation Raleigh.

> This was a suggestion for a memorial plaque to honour a young Lucayan girl whose remains were found in an underwater burial site in the Lucayan National Park.
>
> ◇
>
> ### IN MEMORY OF A YOUNG LUCAYAN GIRL
>
> She was a young maiden of a Lucayan tribe
> who near the hammock caverns did survive
> but at age twelve she died, of a new illness
> and was interred in the blue hole stillness
> a natural skylight above her bell-shaped grave
> atop an underwater talus mound enclave.
>
> For eons undisturbed in her watery mausoleum
> but recently found and displayed in a museum
> but ethics ruled and her remains were re-interred
> in the caverns where her untimely
> demise occurred
> to show dignity to her was the principal concern
> so to this place her remains did rightfully return.
>
> ◇

eager workers ready to provide muscle and skill to help develop the Park. I quickly designed a figure of eight pathway system and suggested locations for a footbridge and visitor centre. The latter two elements I never thought would get built. I was wrong on both counts. The footbridge was constructed mainly through the force of personality of Freeporter, David Knowles. A Visitor Centre was later started but funds ran out. For twenty years I have been trying to get the project re-started. But all in all it was a gratifying achievement on the part of everybody who assisted. To honour the Venturers a new foot bridge has been named to record their achievement.

The *Young Lucayan Girl* poem makes reference, 'in a new illness', it is quite possible the Lucayan girl died of a disease brought from Europe in the early fifteenth century (very probably measles or smallpox). The underwater burial practice of the Lucayans is almost unique in the annals of human archaeology. The Lucayans believed that cave openings like this were the entry to the underworld from which they came and to which they would one day return. The Lucayan National Park underwater cave system entered from the cave openings is among the longest in the world.

Of the National Parks in the Bahamas— Three Are in the Freeport Area

To date, the Bahamas National Trust park system includes 25 national land and sea parks across The Bahamas. They include: Walker's Cay National Park, Black Sound Cay National Reserve, Tilloo Cay Reserve, Pelican Cays Land and Sea Park, Abaco National Park, **Lucayan National Park, Rand Nature Centre, Peterson Cay National Park**, The Retreat, Central Andros National Park Areas, Bonefish Pond National Park, Harrold and Wilson Ponds, Primeval Forest, Exuma Cays Land and Sea Park, Conception Island National Park, Moriah Har-

Entrance to the Burial Mound Cave at the Lucaya National Park.

> Voices cry out in trees, and fingers beckon
> The wings of a million butterflies are sunlight eyes
> There is no sword
> In the enchanted wood
> Branches bend over like a terror,
> The sun has darkened,
> The white wind and the sun and curling wave
> Cradle the coral shore and the tall forest.
> Trees crash at midnight unpredicted,
> Voices cry out
> Naked they walk, and yet with no fear,
> In the strange isle, the wise and gentle.

The blank verse poem above was written by English poet Michael Roberts and is called *In the Strange Isle*. It is a curiously apt work describing an island much like Grand Bahama possibly at the time when the Lucayan Indians inhabited the Bahamas. I first brought attention to the verse in 'Bahama Saga' and suggested that Roberts could have easily have been describing somewhere like the Lucayan National Park.

bour Cay National Park, Marine Farm, Hope House, Inagua National Park, Union Creek, and Little Inagua National Park.

The following excerpt on hurricanes is extracted from an appendix in *Grand Bahama* and concerns the vicious hurricanes experienced in Freeport early in the twenty first century. Though not planned, I left the island the day before the first hurricane hit. Since it was common knowledge a hurricane was on the way I visited the Lucayan National Park and left a cardboard sign on the bridge reading "Bridge Closed." The sign, and much else of course, was blown away in the following days.

The Hurricanes of the New Millenium

Grand Bahama was fortunate to have had relatively few direct hits by hurricanes in the twentieth century. But, as if to equilibrate the landfall statistics, the island suffered the effects of four major hurricanes before the twenty-first century was less than six years old.

In the autumn of 2004 Grand Bahama was hit by two major hurricanes in the space of three weeks. The first was Hurricane *Frances* that followed the almost customary route, heading northwest from the vicinity of the Turks and Caicos Islands and bringing its powerful winds and rain to the eastern Bahamas. After turning west near Abaco it was forecast to hit Freeport on Friday afternoon the 3rd September. Predictably the winds started in the morning and by noon the centre of Freeport had lost electrical power. The radio news reported it as a Category 2 storm that was 300 miles wide with a clearly definable eye some 60 miles across. It was actually much worse than the category number suggests.

At 3am in the morning the police used bull-horns to warn downtown residents to evacuate to higher ground. Not an easy task on an island that has precious little land over 50ft high! Experience of other storms suggested the flooding would come from the Little Bahama Bank to the north and would flood the airport (including the old airport terminal) but stop close to the Grand Bahama Highway. Heeding this many residents stayed where they were. The following morning the weather was nasty but not much worse than a severe rainstorm. Many people thought the worst was over until they had heard on their battery-powered radios that the eye of the storm was directly over Freeport and that the same or worse was to come. In fact it was worse and soon winds picked up coming from the opposite direction. For the next 36 hours the stalled hurricane battered the island. Even the radio station went off the air. By Sunday the hurricane moved away leaving a path of destruction in its wake. One eye-witness said it looked as if the island had experience a blitzkrieg or an ice storm. Everything appeared to be uprooted, twisted and burned. Hardly a leaf remained on the few trees left standing.

But there can be no doubt that the West End community suffered the worst. Besides losing all essential services, trees were uprooted and buildings damaged due to the hurricane force winds the low-lying settlement was flooded to a depth of four feet and more. Hardly a single building escaped the flooding. The view of West End after the storm was a picture of total devastation like something like a WWI battlefield. Sadly one person was drowned.

People on the island soon found the greatest hardship was the lack of power, telephone and running water, and for some, stored food and fuel for vehicles started to run out. Like the proverbial foolish virgins, for these people things were grim indeed. The US Coastguard brought in massive airlifts of water and both of Freeport's icehouses were under police protection with distribution of ice carefully controlled for essential users. As people started to emerge from shelters there were stories of extensive damage to buildings, beach erosion and everywhere downed power and telephone lines snaked the roads. And, as might be expected, there are too few workmen to make urgent repairs and there was a scarcity of building materials anyway.

A strange aftermath of the storm cued the lobsters to make their annual march to deep water. Some people were able to feast on lobster even though there was little to garnish them and no electrical power to cook with. Businesses, banks and offices were badly hit and most were closed for weeks. The local chicken farm lost 400,000 chickens while the shrimps of the flooded shrimp farm found their way back, appropriately perhaps, to the ocean. But slowly the community pulled itself together and for some there were hoots of joy as the power returned 14 days after *Frances* had menaced the northern Bahamas and turned its attention to Florida.

But for many candlelight was still the norm. It was estimated that 1200 power poles had come down though most were replaced by the time some more ominous news was broadcast. It was now the third week after the hurricane and there was news that a new storm—

Hurricane *Jeanne*—had pirouetted about in the Atlantic and was now taking aim on Grand Bahama… A sick joke of the time was that lightning does not strike in the same place twice, though some Jeremiahs were saying that it was the Wrath of God that was being brought to bear upon a wayward nation. For whatever reason Hurricane *Jeanne* bore down on the island. By this time many people had removed their hurricane shutters and started to make repairs. It was commonly thought that only the southwest quadrant of *Jeanne* would affect Freeport. But, sometime during Friday night two weeks after *Frances* the storm ravaged the island and power all over the island went out once more.

The wind veered to the west and increased in intensity. The noise and force of the wind was estimated at 135 mph and was sustained for nearly five hours with wind gusts up to 165 mph! One person explained it as being like standing in a downpour behind a jet engine at full power. The rain was being blown horizontally—and sometimes upwards—so that it entered buildings under the eaves and over the top of sliding doors and debris from the last hurricane was now being re-used as missiles by the storm to break windows and smash into roofs and cars. There were many stories of people seeing plate glass windows and doors buckling inwards with the force of the wind. Sometimes they shattered with frightening effect allowing the driving rain and wind to create havoc inside the buildings. And, as if this were not enough, there was waist high seawater in low-lying areas, and new fresh water lakes in others, flooding buildings in some cases (like Queens Cove)—to a depth of 7 feet!

At the harbour ships in the dry dock were rapidly re-floated and secured to the dock. Even so, one cruise ship under repair broke loose and crushed a tug between itself and the seawall so that the tug sank. By Sunday morning the wind dropped to gale force. Amazingly *Jeanne* had been an even more severe hurricane than *Frances* (it had already taken 100 lives in Haiti). And so the business of clearing up after the hurricane began afresh. Power trucks from Florida, Georgia and even Canada arrived and performed a superb effort to re-establish power.

Lucayan National Park beach after the hurricanes of 2004 showing the uprooted casuarina trees, and the seaweed detritus that contained many sponges.
Note: not a leaf was left on the trees.

Downed trees were sawed up and carted away together with hundreds of tons of debris and people started to put their lives together again. Never, in living memory, had the island suffered as badly as in the hurricanes of '04.

As if the two hurricanes of 2004 were not enough the following year the island was grazed by the infamous Hurricane *Katrina* and received a major hit from Hurricane *Wilma* in October. *Wilma* was stationary over Eight Mile Rock and West End for some 12 hours as a category 3 storm causing very severe damage. (Interestingly this year saw the most named storms on record. The whole alphabet was used up and names had to be found for another four storms). The wind damage was considerable unhappily up-rooting many of the trees that had been replanted from the two previous hurricanes. There was a fair amount of damage to buildings and many tiles were blown from roofs. But the most significant damage was from flooding. Exceptionally high seas were experienced all the way from Silver Point westwards. The sea flooded inland for two hundred yards in places along the coastal land at Eight Mile Rock. Many houses were washed away and simply disappeared while sand, rocks and other debris was deposited far inland.

Lucayan National Park beach after the hurricanes of 2004 showing the uprooted casuarina trees, and the seaweed detritus that contained many sponges. Note: not a leaf was left on the trees.

Postscript

More than two weeks after *Jeanne* had left for Florida the island still looked like a battlefield. The Power Company had spent $12 million in replacing lines and poles and the cost of the hurricanes was tentatively estimated (under-estimated?) at $100 million. Arriving at the new airport terminal it was evident that at least two feet of water had flowed through the building that had been built six or more feet higher than the previous terminal. The old terminal was in ruins and already a start had been made on its demolition. The control tower was clearly badly damaged with most of its windows blown out and boarded up. US Customs personnel had taken a hiatus and all the airport shops were closed and a slow start was being made on renovating premises that had only been open for a month or so. Travelling into Freeport damage to trees was immediately evident. Most of the large ficus trees, despite their giant size and impressive aerial prop root system, had been toppled, the few Norfolk pines had been denuded of branches a looked like totem poles and many of the Caribbean pines in the pine barren had been snapped like match sticks, yet palm trees generally had withstood the storm well. Many shrubs, especially the imported exotics, had disappeared without leaving a trace. But leaves were starting to make an appearance on the trees left standing, in many cases growing straight out of the denuded branches and trunks.

Of the buildings, most with flat roofs, suffered severe water damage and many flat roofs were partly ripped off. Pantile roofs fared badly and hip and ridge tiles in particular suffered damage. Only the metal roofs seemed to have come through the storm unscathed. The conventional wisdom that metal buildings were the strongest was poignantly disproved by the Freeport YMCA and Fire Station that were both severely damaged.

Outside of Freeport the damage from the hurricanes was worse. West End still looked like a muddy battlefield. Clearly the community had received sustained double punches of seawater flooding and wind damage. The Buccaneer Club at Deadman's Reef lost its roof and the seaward side was deluged by blown sand. The flooding had been so bad that the owner had knocked holes in the walls to let the water out. The painted surfaces on the southern exposure of the Buccaneer Club had been completely sand-blasted clean by wind-borne beach sand. The Seagrape Church of St Agnes surprisingly was still standing though it had lost part of its roof sheathing. The priest's residence was not so fortunate—the whole roof had been blown off. At the Lucayan National Park the pedestrian bridge miraculously remained upright but wobbled precariously and was obviously structurally unsound. The southern portion of the bridge was underwater and much of the bridge had lost its handrail (the bridge was replaced in 2009). The mangrove boardwalk had clearly been under 2 or 3 feet of water and almost everywhere had 'floated' off its supports. Standing water was everywhere suggesting that the pathways should be raised or built on higher ground in future. The beach was badly eroded and nearly all the casuarina trees on the beach strand had been blown down their roots creating a continuous 'giant 'hedge'.

Turning to the human side of the disaster, it was interesting to note that camaraderie had developed among Grand Bahamians. Though many people sustained considerable, and often, uninsured losses, there was some small comfort in the fact they were still alive and that 'so-and-so' had had it much worse…

Hurricanes are not the worst problem. Though much more rare, tornados often associated with hurricanes, are several magnitudes worse. The Bahamian Building Codes address the effects of a Category

3 hurricane but do little to mitigate the effects of a tornado. Some time ago I made a proposal for all new construction in the Bahamas to contain a small 'safe' room, something like a closet or bathroom with reinforced walls and an internal 'roof" that would be so designed to resist the extreme wind force of a tornado assuming the rest of the fabric of the building was destroyed. Obviously it would cost a little more but it would undoubtedly save lives—and that is something one cannot put a price on!

Edward St. George

Co-chairman of the Port Authority

16 November 1998

To: Mr Edward St George

Dear Edward

It is a long time since I addressed you on a subject about which, I am sure you know, I feel very strongly: namely the Lucayan National Park. Many people, myself included, consider that the land to the east of the Park—if there were any justice in the world—should be conserved for benefit of future generations and not leased for housing/resort development which cannot fail to do serious ecological damage to the delta of Gold Rock Creek. Whether the Bahamas National Trust is the right custodian for the land is not the issue, I simply believe the land should be conserved.

Michael Albury the regional director of the National Trust has been good enough to share some information with me on the changing nature of the development proposals but I confess I have not seen an up-to-date plan of their proposal and I should further state the opinions expressed in this letter are my own and not those of the Trust.

I understand Footprints have (predictably) changed their original intentions from providing housing units dropped in by helicopter, to conventional construction presumably entailing strip foundations and concrete pads; their earlier proposal of eco-sensitive servicing of the units with biodegradable waste disposal etc. is to be substituted by more conventional methods for 118 units which I believe could mean 118 septic tanks or the equivalent in a central sewage treatment plant or plants (only a token 10 cabins I understand will now have eco-sensitive composting units); the original provision of boardwalks has now been

This letter was written to the then Co-Chairman of the Port Authority. It concerned the proposal to build a series of bungalows on a narrow strip of land sandwiched between Gold Rock Creek and the sea.

superseded by narrow paved roads (the developer would probably prefer to substitute a euphemism for 'roads'); and I understand the original proposal for a wooden bridge crossing Gold Rock Creek has now been changed in favour of a bridge to be constructed of reinforced concrete plumb in the middle of the mangroves. I am further told there is also a new proposal for two piers extending from the rocky foreshore into the sea. The piers, I understand, are not for boats (which is bad enough) but for floating house-boats or what the developer calls 'boat house type facilities for guest functions'. So one can possibly add the equivalent of another ten or so units to the total unit count and increase the possibility of sea pollution by a factor of 5. I am also informed (or misinformed) that for the privilege of helping destroy the most exquisite tract of land on Grand Bahama they are paying only a peppercorn rent to the Development Company.

I understand government have sensibly requested an Environmental Impact Study and hopefully this will give all parties time to review their positions. The proposed development would certainly appear to be contrary to the spirit of the new Wetlands Act if not in direct conflict with it. I will now list several specific objections I have to the proposal:

First, I do not think there should be any development whatsoever on the dunes. This strand is presently subject to severe erosion by the sea. Personal knowledge of this area suggests that the sea has claimed up to 50ft of foreshore in two decades. The beach strand is almost certainly the site of a Lucayan village, evidence of which was unearthed by Dr Granberry and myself a few years back. If development proceeds on the unprotected beach shoreline I anticipate in a very short time there will be encroachment by the sea necessitating the building of sea walls or other structures to protect the buildings. The actual construction of the units and the concomitant clearing of the site will only accelerate the erosion. And this says nothing of the aesthetic harm permanent human presence will inflict on a pristine beach.

Second, I do not know enough about Footprints current servicing or waste disposal plans but let us not forget the development will sit directly above the unique and extensive labyrinth of the Lucayan Caverns. Any disposal wells, trenches, bridge abutments, septic/holding tanks, sewage treatment plants and foundations may puncture the caverns and introduce pollution which could corrupt the whole cavern system. This needs to be studied very, very carefully.

Three, the service 'roads' cannot help but destroy many acres of the most sensitive vegetation along the ironshore and beach strand. Many more acres will be destroyed by the construction of an access road and bridge in the middle of Gold Rock Creek and the most extensive and beautiful mangrove forest on the south side of the island.

Four, provision of utilities to service the project cannot fail to further damage the eco-system. Heavy equipment to trench for the water and power lines (an overhead power distribution system is of course out of the question on aesthetic grounds) will destroy a swath of vegetation at least 15 feet wide. In short, together with the building pads for 128 units it will virtually take out most of the critical sea-margin vegetation between the mangroves and the sea. The main utility feeder lines to the development will either have to go through the swash or have to cross the mouth of the Creek. Both options in my opinion could be disastrous.

Five, the new proposal of building two piers from the rocky foreshore for 'boat house facilities' certainly needs clarification (see above). The piers may not in themselves be traumatic to the environment but it forebodes a greater problem: boats. The presence of residents in this area means that the boats will have to be moored somewhere. Some may end up being lifted from the water and parked on Footprints land. Many more, I suggest will be moored (and choke) the mouth of the Creek. Even if specifically denied by Agreement, in time of storm they cannot reasonably be denied access to the Creek. Then smaller boats, inevitably, will travel up the Creek to the further detriment of wildlife, the environment and the Lucayan National Park which is already near saturation point. (Incidentally the most extensive 'pier' on the island is already located at the south-eastern corner marker of the site).

A final thought. Experience from my 30 years in the practice of planning in the Bahamas suggests that the ethical intentions of developers often get lost when business considerations are taken into account. For instance if, once the project is operating and Code enforcement or contractual obligations are invoked, the developer may honestly state that he cannot comply without affecting employment. This establishes a dangerous dichotomy between the livelihood of Bahamians and the environment in which the latter will certainly loose. In short without exceptional controls and monitoring, this development promises to portend a catastrophe. In my opinion the realisation of this project will be the antithesis of the democratic dictum of the 'greatest good for the greatest number.'

Edward I do not have to tell you how strongly I feel about this issue. Just as Freeport is turning a corner it seems such a pity that a slough of swashland may come to haunt your stewardship. There are many areas of land on the island where eco-sensitive development should be the only option, the problem is, this site is not one of them. Not to minimise your achievements but there was a certain inevitability about the eventual expansion of the harbour and increasing the number of hotel rooms but to selflessly preserve something major like a tract of wetland containing a unique and diverse ecosystem for posterity would indeed be a statesmanlike

```
gesture and a tribute to what I know is your care
and concern for the Bahamas.
   I would be happy to discuss this matter with you
further and can be reached at the telephone numbers
given above.
   Isabelle joins me in sending her love and kind
regards to you and Henrietta.

   Yours etc.,

   Peter Barratt
```

We won! Edward St. George graciously accepted the arguments and the project was abandoned.

Some of us wrote a similar polemic to the *Freeport News* editor about the awful great hole that the film crew of *Pirates of the Caribbean* excavated and then (predictably) abandoned near the mouth of Gold Rock Creek.

TIDAL VIGILANCE

Since a rising tide raises all boats
consider well and take careful note
spring and neap or shallow and deep
in one you paddles in t'other you float.

FILM COLONY DEBACLE

Remember how the film colony at Gold Rock was promoted as a great asset to the island? Well, not for the first time, the extravagant praise lauded on a new project in Grand Bahama was ill founded. The project actually got off on the wrong foot when it was not clear that all the approvals were in place. But that turned out to be the least of the problems. In no time the film colony had destroyed the aquifer that New Freetown relied upon for its potable water supply. Also access to a public beach was virtually denied. Then they set about destroying the mangroves adjacent to the mouth of Gold Rock Creek—in possibly the most scenic inland area of the island. Next came massive dredging excavations that produced a moon landscape now occupied with a hodge podge of trailers and heavy equipment. What ever happened to the charming old world film sets of pirate haunts most of us visualized? But worse, much worse, was to follow. The dredging was conducted in such a manner that the run-off produced major turbidity in the inshore waters. This turbidity invaded possibly the finest reef on the island with dire results. It is doubtful the reef will survive. So the island gained employment for a few truck drivers and heavy equipment operators, the government presumably gained a license fee but we lost another part of Paradise.

Concerned Bahamian

This letter was not half as interesting as the reply it triggered in the *Freeport News*.

Bahamas Film Studio Praised

Dear Editor,

I was born and raised in The Bahamas and am proud to say that I work for the Bahamas Film Studio. In response to the letter in your paper written by persons unknown, claiming to be a concerned Bahamian, I would like to make it clear that not one single word of this slanderous criticism bears even a distant resemblance to the truth.

The first lie states that work began before the appropriate permits were in place. Horse Hockey! No work was undertaken without the expressed written consent of the government. No further comment on this matter is required. It's just not true.

The individual then states that "the colony" destroyed the aquifer supplying New Freetown's fresh water. Rotten Apples!

Not only did the construction have zero negative impact on any fresh water supply, but in fact several hundred yards of contaminated soils were excavated and removed to the proper land fill site at significant expense to the studio. Furthermore, at the insistence of studio management, Dr. Richard Cant, the world's foremost authority on lime rock island aquifers, came to the site and confirmed that the studio's project could not possibly have any ill effect on the fresh water supply. However, the residents on the beach road have been provided with pressurized, purified, filtered fresh water, piped to their door at no charge. May I also comment that not a single one of these individuals is a citizen of this country, yet they are treated with the utmost respect and concern by the studio. Regarding beach access, if it's required that rubber-neckers and paparazzi can't walk this small section of the beach while filming is in progress, what's wrong with that?

The writer suggests that another part of paradise has been lost. Which part was that? The part where the jet and diesel fuel tank farm stood, leaking hydrocarbons into the sand for 50 years? Or was it the part where the U.S. military had buried old vehicles and scrap metal adjacent to the mangroves? Didn't anybody ever wonder why nothing grew there?

Well now it's clean. Guess who paid for that. As far as the moonscape as a result of the excavations, it's a construction site that has yet to be completed. When it's finished, the beach in that area will be covered in indigenous plant life, like palms and sea grape, not Casurinas imported from Australia which have continually caused erosion throughout our country.

So the island gained a few jobs for truck drivers! What a ridiculous comment. How dim-witted, obtuse and misleading. There are more than 450 real Bahamians at work as a result of this project. Most of us are making more money than we have ever made in our lives. I am a professional lobster fisherman, but have been starving for the last few years as a result of three major hurricanes destroying the reefs from Grand Bahama to Orange Cay. My shelters were lost, and the reefs covered with sand and silt. That's where the damage came from, hurricanes. When you have spent as much time on the ocean floor as I have, then you'd know what you're talking about. It's obvious you do not.

So before you start attacking what many of us see as a godsend, ask the more than 100 taxi drivers how anxious they are to go back to lining up at the airport in hopes of making a few dollars to feed their families. Ask the hundred or more cooks and cleaners and security people how much of a hurry they are in to go back to waiting for the Royal Oasis to reopen. Ask the 30 or so boat captains how much they want to go back to sea, for weeks at a time in weather you have only seen in the movies. All this just so they can face death 50 ways you never dreamed of. For once Bahamians are not dependent on the tourist dollar and don't have to rely on tips to put bread on the table.

I want to thank the government and the studio for the fabulous opportunities we working men and women have been offered. I also thank God for bringing them both together at this time and place. Shame on the writer of that thoughtless article who hides behind the pen name of a concerned Bahamian. This country was not created just for you.

Sincerely,
A Proud, Real Bahamian

A month or so after this letter was published (presumably the writer had a lot 'help' from the Film Colony management in writing it—Bahamian lobster fishermen do not normally use that kind of terminology!) the site was abandoned as predicted, and the writer is now presumably back catching lobsters...

> The Bahamas Film Studios at Gold Rock Creek continue to be a marvelous resource for us, arguably boasting the world's largest "Open Water Tank" *(read: hole in the ground)*, it will provide production companies with state-of-the-art production facilities to satisfy the most demanding project...

Late in 2007 the Bahamas Film Commission wrote the above letter. In 2011 it was still awaiting a 'most demanding project'...!

Recently there has been a lot of argument
about the Confederacy and attendant sentiment
I can't see a problem today—
they lost didn't they?

LETTERS

Since I have lived part of my life in Miami it is only natural that I should have taken an interest in happenings in South Florida as recorded in the local newspaper, the *Miami Herald*. I have included below some of the notes and letters I sent to the *Herald* almost all of them unpublished.

In autumn of 1984 *The Herald* published a series of excellent, though negative, articles about the Bahamas entitled: 'A Nation for Sale—Corruption in the Bahamas'. The series of articles coincided with the Commonwealth Prime Minister's Conference that was being held in Nassau. Even though the excellent investigative reporting clearly pointed to wrong-doing by the Lynden Pindling-led government, its findings were soon brushed aside and the Bahamian prime minister and his party managed to survive in office for 25 years. I took a special interest in this as I have lived half a lifetime in the islands. Most of the following letters make reference to the Bahamas.

Interestingly the Nassau *Tribune* formed a liaison with the *Miami Herald* presumably but unsuccessfully, to give readers in the Bahamas a world perspective. It clearly did not work and the association was soon dropped.

The *Miami Herald* articles about corruption in the Bahamas were followed by the *Sunday Times* of London that devoted its magazine section of 29 September 1985 in an attempted exposé of Sir Lynden Pindling and his associates.

The Deputy Prime Minister, A. D. Hanna until then a stalwart adversary of foreign immigration resigned saying that he was dismayed at revelations of widespread graft and corruption. (Mr Hanna was later appointed Governor General of The Bahamas, even though he was the personal representative of the British monarch in the Bahamas for reasons most people understood he never accepted the customary knighthood).

The *Report* noted the Prime Minister had received millions of dollars in loans and gifts from foreign businessmen including a large six figure sum from the Chairman of the Grand Bahama Port Authority who declared it was 'a loan which he did not expect would be re-paid'. At this time the respected Hubert Ingraham and Perry Christie both expressed their lack of confidence in the Prime Minister and were summarily dismissed from Cabinet (interestingly both were later to become Prime Ministers of The Bahamas but as heads of different political parties).

Prime Minister Sir Lynden Pindling was eventually exonerated of wrong-doing by the Commission (significantly the future Anglican Bishop of the Bahamas deferred with a minority opinion) but two ministers in the PLP Cabinet, Kendall Nottage (then a resident of Freeport) and George Smith, resigned after the Commission was severely critical of their conduct.

LETTER TO THE EDITOR:

ELECTIONS IN THE BAHAMAS

While the *Miami Herald* carries news of Cuba daily on almost every page an overlooked country not 50 miles from our shores has demonstrated once again what true democracy is all about. On May 2, 2002 Bahamians went to the polls and elected a new government. The change of government is not so significant as how change was effected. The former government called an election just three months ago as a kind of vote of confidence—and lost. We were spared talking heads prattling on about an election over twelve months away as on all the major US networks. Neither party in The Bahamas was so funded that it could trounce its opponent in what must be the weakest aspect of American democracy. It is customary for about 90% of the electorate to vote in The Bahamas (the US figure hovers around 50%), and votes have to be collected from islands occupying an area the size of Italy. Yet the results were collated in about 12 hours and broadcast to the nation. The former Prime Minister graciously conceded defeat. And, even though rhetoric was intense, few incidents were reported. Another thing about Bahamian-style democracy is that if the new Prime Minister does not perform as hoped for, he can be replaced at any time during his 5-year term by his peers (you will recall this is what happened to Margaret Thatcher but unhappily did not happen to George Bush). And one last matter concerns the judiciary: Bahamians would consider it absolute madness to have politicians appoint judges. In the Bahamas the most qualified professionals are appointed to the Bench—even if this means employing foreign nationals! If Americans had any humility they could learn a lot politically from the small island nation of The Bahamas.

~Peter Barratt

> **FROM THE DESK OF:**
> **Peter Barratt**
>
> GO BACK TO TEXAS
>
> So Patricia Rodriguez doesn't like the charming little island of Green Turtle Cay in the Bahamas and the *Miami Herald* obligingly gives her the front page of the *Travel Section* to enumerate her dislikes! So there are creepy crawlies in the tropics, on small islands they don't have a Winn Dixie supermarket and yes, the light sometimes goes out and, though she doesn't say it, she found she hasn't got much in common with the native people, black or white, either. She should not be surprised. While in Green Turtle Cay I wonder how many times she started a sentence with, 'well in Texas we. . .' So she is now going to the Dominican Republic. I expect we have to look forward to another predicable essay on the primitive folks down there. The *Herald* would do well to suggest that she, her letters and her prejudices, go back to Texas.

A Texan expatriate wrote a letter denigrating Green Turtle Cay that the *Miami Herald* was happy to publish on the front page of the Travel Section. The above is what I wrote (it was not published of course).

FROM THE DESK OF:
Peter Barratt

What an interesting article on the front page of the *Herald* about ancient crocodiles and things in The Bahamas! It has long been known that crocodiles existed in the blue holes of The Bahamas but never has evidence of them been found in such numbers. Your readers might be interested to know that the Lucayan Indians (the people that Columbus first met when he came to the Bahamas) practiced a strange form of underwater burial and evidence of this has been found in many underwater caves in the islands. About twenty years ago, in the caves of Grand Bahama *Spelionectes lucayensis*, a previously unknown crustacean, that looks like a swimming centipede was found. The small creature now forms a new class of marine life. Also Ponce de Leon took note of the water-filled caverns in the Bahamas and that is probably why he left two men on Grand Bahama Island to look for the *Fountain of Youth*. The underwater caves on Grand Bahama incidentally were once the longest charted underwater cave system in the world.

PS. To read more about the caves of the Bahamas the reader might like to refer to Rob Palmer's excellent book 'Blue Holes of The Bahamas.' Also the National Geographic magazine in 2010 included an article on Bahamian blue holes. Less important perhaps are two books I wrote about the Bahamas and sent for your library: 'Grand Bahama' and 'Bahama Saga' that mention, among other things, Bahamian blue holes.

The letter above I wrote had an inexcusably self-serving postscript that fairly guaranteed it would not be published.

The following letter was written in reply to an Editorial in the *Miami Herald* over a spat that occurred between the Bahamas and the US (abetted by the Miami Cuban community) over some dentists who escaped from Cuba and entered the Bahamas illegally. The sub-title of the *Herald* editorial was *'Our opinion: straddling the fence is poor foreign policy'.* In accordance with an agreement with Cuba the Bahamas intended to return them to their homeland. For most of the time since Castro came to power the United States has had an embargo on Cuba, it has also an immigration policy that favours Cubans over other nationalities. This has been made possible because of a powerful and vindictive expatriate Cuban lobby in Washington.

The conclusion to the situation was a compromise. The dentists were released to a third country and from there made their way to Miami (of course). An editorial in the *Miami Herald* expressed exasperation that the Bahamas would not release the Cuban dentists to the United States as requested.

People who treat every day as their last might,

No...will,

one day ... be right !

April 17, 2006

The Bahamas: Pinched by Neighbors

True, it is not easy to try to steer a middle course between bickering neighbours but surely it is laudable to attempt a middle way. Your editorial April 17, 2002 would suggest otherwise. To make the case as to why the Bahamas should side with the United States your editorial utilizes some muddled thinking comparing the situation to US involvement in two World Wars. True, after entering the wars (over two years late in both cases) they were costly in terms of money and lives lost but nobody surely doubts it was right thing to do! There was ethically no other choice and it was anyway, in America's interest to defeat international tyranny.

The real drift of your argument becomes clear when you illustrate your case with the Cuban dentist detention saga. Everyone knows that US policy in the Caribbean region is Cuban exile-driven (and perhaps even the editorial policy of some Miami newspapers!) Sovereign independent democratic countries (and you admit the Bahamas is one of them) can and must follow their own interests and obey their international agreements. As you say, the choice is easy—and so it is. The Bahamas should not acquiesce to the arrogance and bullying of a larger neighbour, especially when it is upholding the terms of an international agreement. Might is not always right. ∎

The Big Stick

Sometimes because Americans carry a big stick, they forget, or simply choose not to walk softly when it comes to dealing with countries and people that are seen to them to be insignificant. This perhaps is the position of the two Congress representatives who propose to call for sanctions against The Bahamas, if their wishes are not met expeditiously in having two detained Cuban nationals at the Carmichael Road Detention Centre, handed over to the Americans.

The Bahamas' man in Washington, Joshua Sears, gave just the right response when he said that sanctions against this country would be a losing situation for both countries, and would do much to impair the good relationship between The Bahamas and the United States, with particular respect to drug interdiction and migration. There is no question that The Bahamas has been responsive to the Americans in the execution of the extradition initiatives and over the years numerous Bahamian nationals and others have been extradited to face charges in the U.S.

Perhaps the U.S. Congressman, Connie Mack and Congresswoman Ileana Ros-Lehtinen are looking narrowly at The Bahamas being a small country and that if the U.S. wants the Cubans released to them, they should get them, case closed. In effect they are saying, give us what we want or face the consequences: We'll take out our pre-clearance facilities; we'll make it rough on your tourist industry; we'll do this to you and we'll do that. If you go against us, we'll crush you.

They are waving their big stick in the face of The Bahamas in a most threatening manner, which cannot

The above was an editorial article that appeared in a local paper concerning the Cubans who had escaped from Cuba and had been detained in the Bahamas.

be appreciated by the citizens of this country.

This is certainly not being the good neighbour and friend that we say they are. This is definitely more in line with the big, strong and powerful bully taking unfair advantage of the small, independent neighbour, who dares to have a difference of opinion.

The Bahamas is a friend and trading partner of the United States as well as it enjoys diplomatic relations and treaty concessions with Cuba. It is unfair and it is wrong for The Bahamas to be put into a position of making a choice between those two countries, because they can't talk to each other. The one choice The Bahamas has—the right choice—is to return the two Cuban nationals to Cuba. That is the agreement and if it is not honoured, The Bahamas will have a difficult time sitting around a negotiating table and holding its head up anywhere in this region, or in the world.

But Foreign Affairs Minister Fred Mitchell feels that "wiser counsel" (than the two Congress representatives) would suggest that to bring economic pressure on The Bahamas would not be in the best interest of the south Florida communities which greatly benefit from the "mutually important bilateral relationship between us."

It may not be an easy matter to resolve, however, it is incumbent upon Minister Mitchell and the government to ensure that the agreed conventions are adhered to and that what is right is done in the best interest of the Bahamian people.■

LETTER TO THE EDITOR:

What Jose Sanchez (letter to the *Miami Herald*) does not understand is that the Bahamas has, proportionately, an even greater illegal immigration problem than the United States. The sad fact is that Haitians and Cubans are escaping from failed states and their reason for so doing is actually, and understandably, economic. The Bahamas does the best it can with limited resources but remember it has suffered three devastating hurricanes recently (2004/6). If Senor Sanchez now chooses not to visit the Bahamas—then it is his loss.

The letter above was written in response to a letter by a Mr Jose Sanchez who was angry at the Bahamas government for detaining the Cubans who arrived in the Bahamas illegally. Most countries send illegals back to the country they came from. In this case the Bahamas made an exception and let the Cubans continue on to travel.... to where you can guess!

LETTER TO THE EDITOR:

THE BAHAMAS SHOWS HOW TO HAVE FAIR ELECTIONS

Seven hundred Bahamian islands spread over an area the size of Italy went to the polls on May 2, 2002 to choose a new parliamentary government. The pre-election rhetoric was fierce but generally good-natured and the party-like election rallies featured would-be politicians often with their own catchy song accompaniment. One exception perhaps was the Bishop who told his congregation if they did not vote for the party he supported they could find another church!

The incumbent Free National Movement party had presided over 10 years of unprecedented prosperity in the Bahamas. So confident were they that they held a referendum a few months before the election to enshrine more rights for women. Prime Minister Hubert Ingraham, a popular grass-roots politician, prophesied that who ever won the referendum would win the election. He was right. The referendum was defeated and his party lost out to the Progressive Liberal Party of the left of the political spectrum.

At the election over 90% of the registered voters cast their vote. The election machinery was a model of transparency. Everyone eligible to vote had to register for photographic ID cards. At the polling booths the voting card was checked with representatives of the political parties looking on. To make doubly sure that no one voted twice each voter had to dip the whole of his or her right thumb in a poisonous looking purple indelible ink. Then, just before voting, the voting procedure was orally explained to each voter. Basically they were told to put an 'X' by the candidate of their choice and nothing more. This they did behind a small screen. Once completed they folded the card in two and deposited the card into the ballot box in full public view.

> Less than four hours after the votes had been counted the local television and radio stations announced all the results from the far-flung islands. The election result was a complete reversal of the previous election. This time the PLP won by a landslide: out of 40 contested seats the PLP won 29, the FNM gained a mere 7 and Independents won another 4.
>
> At the polling stations there were no armed police or military present, no roster of choices for dog-catchers or nit-picky social issues and no complex machines with ill-fitting punch cards and hanging chads. No, the Bahamian election was a model for all would-be democracies.
>
> Former president Jimmy Carter was right to stay away.
>
> Peter Barratt

I sent a copy of the letter above to the Prime Minister Christie together with my book 'Grand Bahama' but the gesture was unacknowledged. Later I also sent copies of my book to the Prime Minister Ingraham and some of his ministers in the FNM government and to Arthur Hanna when he was Governor General (a retail value of $125). They too did not see fit to reply. Equal opportunity snubs!

Decline of the *Miami Herald*

It must be clear by now one of my least favourite newspapers in the world is the *Miami Herald*. It is sad because it used to be one of the great regional newspapers of America. I have to admit their photographers and illustrators are good but most of the best articles are borrowed from other news sources. The most interesting part of the paper for me are the letters which of course are written by people other than *Miami Herald* staff.

The paper is still circulated widely in Latin America, the Caribbean and the Bahamas but has now seemingly been hijacked by the powerful Miami-Cuban majority and serves as their mouthpiece. To be fair it has all the problems that newsprint has in the world today: falling readership and shrinking advertising (though viewing the 2lb the Sunday edition that is hard to believe).

At weekends and holidays the useful newsprint occupies less than 25% of the paper, the remainder being highly coloured largely unread advertising flyers. The *Herald* uses its good reporters, and there are a few of them, on stories that keep up a barrage of negativity about the (admittedly) awful state of affairs in mainland Cuba. Occasionally it strays off that subject and prints other stories that are also well off course. One particular piece seemed to use the words democracy and republican interchangeably. Here is how I responded:

LETTER TO THE EDITOR:

REPUBLICS AND DEMOCRACIES—are not the same thing!

They are often used—especially in the American press—as being almost synonymous.

But are they ?

One dictionary definition of a republic, (taken from the *American Heritage Dictionary* who you would think would know better), records that a 'republic is any political order that is not a monarchy (and has) a constitutional form of government, especially a democratic one.'

Really? What an imbecilic definition!

The definition may be true about a republic having some form of constitution but it is dead wrong about it is being '...especially a democratic one.' This clearly is not the case.

Indeed most 'republics' are not 'democratic' in any real sense of the word. Take for example, North Korea, Iran, Libya and many countries in Africa and quite a few in Asia and elsewhere. All have constitutions it is true, but few are generally recognized as 'democratic'.

So what is a democracy? The same dictionary defines the word as: 'government by the people exercised directly or through elected representatives'.

Interestingly it is the countries that the American Heritage Dictionary dismissively refers to as 'monarchies' where one finds that democratic freedoms and practices are strongest. The confusion arises perhaps because no distinction is made between 'constitutional' and 'absolute' monarchies.

Saudi Arabia is an 'absolute' monarchy; Jordan, Morocco and Nepal (not any more) are something in between. Great Britain is a 'constitutional' monarchy. And so for that matter are Canada, Australia,

Sweden, Netherlands, Belgium, Thailand, Japan, The Bahamas and Spain. The latter country was a republic ruled by a fascist republican dictator for over thirty years before becoming a 'constitutional' monarchy. Since Franco died—and the republic with him—Spain has become a universally-admired progressive modern and democratic country. To a large extent it owes its transformation to an enlightened and well-respected monarchy.

So in summary: if you are looking for a true respected and functioning democracy your best bet is a constitutional monarchy!

I did not get this letter published so I thought I would have another try:

LETTER TO THE EDITOR:

REPUBLIC versus MONARCHY

In the great republic of the United States it has become popular to denigrate countries with a monarchy as somehow backward and anachronistic. It might be well to set the record straight. It was a republic that brought us the holocaust, it was a republic that developed the atomic bomb and used it (twice) on civilian populations, it was two rival republics that gave us over forty years of Cold War, it is a republic in the Middle East that has the biggest stockpile of chemical weapons and WMD in the region (but denies their existence), it is a republic that most threatens the peace of the world by developing a nuclear arsenal on the Korean peninsular, and it is Islamic 'crazies' who live in republics who threaten to create belligerent theocratic republics in Africa and the Middle East.

Monarchies, particularly the constitutional variety, are not perfect but they stand as beacons of hope even in the Middle East. Morocco, Jordan and the Gulf sheikdoms are relatively (2009) progressive states in an unstable region. Even the Saudi Arabian monarchy has been a consistently good friend of the United States even though many of its citizens despise the West. Looking elsewhere, Japan, Australia, New Zealand and Thailand (until recently!) are about the most stable and progressive countries in the Pacific region. In Europe, Sweden, the Netherlands, Norway and the United Kingdom are among the most fair-minded progressive countries in the world. And Spain is perhaps the shining example, having thrown off a republican dictatorship, it is already a highly-respected, forward-looking country with a crowned monarch as head of state. In the Western hemisphere the tiny Falkland Islands has a stable government and economy that is the envy of

Argentina, the English-speaking Caribbean Islands (including Bermuda) acknowledge a monarch as head of state, and are way ahead of their poorer 'republican' neighbors. And the second largest country in the world that, by some counts, is the most respected nation on the globe, happens to recognize a monarch as head of state. That country, of course, is Canada.

And, perhaps unsurprisingly, this wasn't published either!

THE FAR HORIZON

Looking across the far horizon, toward
the barely visible curve of planet earth
across a sea with giant energy stored
all tell of the world's magnitude and girth.
Across this same ocean looking north
where dark waters extend to polar climes
mankind through ages has journeyed forth
enduring perilous passage many times
with fog and iceberg danger never far
all illustrating how brave, yet fragile, we are.

Media

There is no need to say much about the media, since by definition, they speak for themselves. In the early days the national broadcasting service ZNS was the only audio link the country possessed. It was a great event when ZNS opened its northern service in Freeport and later came television supplied by CTV. Private enterprise has since stepped forward and there are several Freeport-based radio stations and a cable service that offers international channels as well as carrying ZNS and local broadcasters. Recently an excellent service started aimed mainly at informing visitors about events and attractions on the island. Though it may be fair to say it is the foreign channels that are most viewed by Freeporters.

The *Freeport News* proudly trumpets on its front page that it is Freeport's first newspaper and is now its only newspaper. (It is actually owned by the *Guardian/Tribune* that suggests something of a monopoly on newsprint in the Bahamas). For a time Pierre Dupuch was the editor of a Freeport-produced edition of the *Grand Bahama Tribune* but the publication folded after a year or two. The facts at this juncture are hard to piece together but it may have had something to do with the independent content of articles in the local *Tribune*.

Media reports intended for the local population in Freeport have always been quite reluctant to take a stand against 'city hall' (specifically the Port Authority). Cynics might wonder if it might have something to do with the Port Authority as an important source of advertising. There are articles galore of course about Freeport and there were almost daily reports on the Port Authority ownership dispute but little critical editorial comment on the situation. Even when the owners paid themselves over $100 million dollars it was reported with hardly a comment. These obscene windfalls—reminiscent of the Wall Street bonus scandal—have almost certainly been expatriated and will not be re-invested in the Bahamas. But for all this there has seldom been an unkind word expressed in editorials about the autocratic Port Authority. It makes one wonder.

Nassau Guardian—Tuesday, August 7, 2001

US Banker Loses Leg in Shark Fight

A New York man celebrating his wedding anniversary in the Bahamas had part of his left leg amputated after being attacked by a shark. Krishna Thompson, 36, a Wall Street banker, was in a critical condition yesterday, a spokeswoman at Jackson Memorial Hospital in Miami said.

His wife, Ave Maria Thompson, told the *Miami Herald*: "He was just swimming off the Lucayan Beach when something, a shark, grabbed his leg and started pulling him down. He kept punching and punching. He has cuts on his hands because of that."

The Thompsons were celebrating their 10th wedding anniversary in Freeport, Grand Bahama. On Saturday Krishna Thompson went alone into the water. After struggling with the shark, Mrs Thompson said, her husband managed to free himself and swam to the shore using only his right leg, because the other was mangled.

Onlookers helped him on to the shore, where he collapsed. His leg was amputated just above the knee.

AP, Miami ∎

I wonder if you recall the news immediately before 9/11? Bet you don't. But it was about a man who lost his leg to a shark bite in Freeport, Bahamas. There is some irony in the event. There was a strange unauthenticated rumour about this event. It was alleged that Mr Thompson worked at the World Trade Center. Just 35 days later, if he had gone to work as normal, he might have lost his life in the WTC collapse. If true, this could have given rise to a sardonic headline: 'Shark saves man's life.'

88 / Freeport Notebook

Hotels on Lucaya Beach. The candy-striped lighthouse of the original hotel, long a symbol of Lucaya, is just visible upper right

POST OFFICE BOX F-4XXX

In most places in the world postmen will deliver mail even if they have to trudge through rain, mud or hail. And, if there is a parcel to bring, they will never fail to dutifully deliver the package as part of their detail. But in Freeport in sullen comfort, no mailman knocks instead, all mail is stuffed into a tiny Post Office Box.

In 2010 the National Geographic magazine had the effrontery to suggest that Freeport was one of the least desirable places in the world to visit as a tourist. Obviously it begged a response. Here it is in prose and verse.

LETTER TO THE EDITOR:

Well Grand Bahama can take comfort from one thing that the self-appointed experts at *National Geographic* reported, if the island is indeed the third from the bottom of worst places to visit, it has only one place to go—and that is up! We might however, call into question the 'expertise' of *National Geographic* in making this harsh pronouncement, after all, it was these same people that in 1992 spent a million dollars on a flawed attempt to propose Samana Cay as the landfall of Columbus!

A POETIC REPLY TO *NATIONAL GEOGRAPHIC*

Criticism from Nat Geographic
caused the island a bit of static
tourist spot blighted they surmised
but we do not need to be surprised
Nat Geo were wrong before you see
touting the landfall site as Samana Cay
when the world knows the landfall really
was at San Salvador, and not just nearly,
...but quite clearly!

Correspondence with President Jimmy Carter

While undertaking research for his novel *The Hornet's Nest* that took seven years to write, President Carter says he just read a line about an old slave but he turned her into a heroine in his book. Simon Schama author of the non-fiction work Rough Crossings, a history of slaves at the time of the American Revolution, writes about the same slave from smidgens of historical information but gives the name of the same slave name as Quamino.

A reviewer noted that one of Carter's more interesting fictional creations was this same slave who, after being raped by the rebels, leads the British by a secret path into Savannah. Carter based the inclusion of the slave incident in his story on a historical footnote describing an unnamed slave as the betrayer of the coastal city. The reviewer continues that some of the minor characters in his book afford a glimpse of real novelistic talent of the former president. Even though Quamino aka Quash Dolly has no more than a walk-on part, she is of such historical interest that one wishes to know more about her. She is capable of speaking English with precision and verve, but hides this behind the thick mumble deemed more suitable by her masters. The reviewer notes her portrait is a triumph of Carter's empathy with a character wholly unlike himself.

Some history books only mention an unnamed slave as the betrayer of the coastal town. Carter and Schama at least give us her name. Interestingly she was freed by the British and taken to Nassau.

Attempts to find what happened to her in Nassau in the Bahamian archives have so far been unsuccessful.

Having found the 'The Hornet's Nest' an intriguing story I thought I should write to President Carter to find out the source of the story.

> 28 February 2004
>
> The Carter Center
> One Copenhill
> 453 Freedom Parkway
> Atlanta, GA 30307
>
> Dear President Carter:
>
> Thank you for your kind note acknowledging the sample chapter I sent you from my forthcoming book 'Bahama Saga'.
>
> Since I last wrote to you I have read *The Hornet's Nest* which I found captivating. As a Bahamian of 'loyalist' persuasions I thought the book was remarkably well balanced in its portrayal of 'loyalist/tory' and 'rebel/whig' Americans.
>
> I was particularly interested in your portrayal of the slave girl 'Quash Dolly' who, in your story, made her way to Nassau in the Bahamas. I wondered if this young lady was completely fictional or was based on an actual character? If the latter, I should be so grateful if you could give me the source of your information.
>
> Thank you for your kind attention. With all good wishes,
>
> Sincerely yours,
>
> Peter Barratt

I was amazed—and gratified—that President Carter would have replied. Here is what he wrote:

> To Peter:
> Thanks, I hope your book does well -
> Best wishes,
> Jimmy

PLANNING

The Components of a City Come Together

The centre of Freeport was laid out by Jan Porel the first town planner. He decreed it should be located half way between the harbour and Pine Ridge. The early buildings were designed by an exceptionally talented architect Alfred Browning Parker a disciple of Frank Lloyd Wright who designed the original airport terminal building, the administration building on Pioneers Way (that later became a Court), the Rand Clinic and two palatial houses on the Lucayan beach. One house was for Jack Hayward the other for Wallace Groves (the latter of which at the time was the largest residence after Government House in the colony). Sadly all these buildings have been demolished or remodeled and provide little hint of the original structure.

The Mercantile Bank building dominated the new city centre and the Port Authority leased the two upper floors. At the harbour the ship bunkering operation worked overtime to bunker ocean-going ships and provide a much needed cash flow to the Port Authority. Also at the harbour a major cement plant was constructed and wharfs were provided for cruise ships. Syntex opened a pharmaceutical plant and near to the

The Groves residence on Lucayan Beach designed by Architect Browning Parker (now demolished)

Bahamas Oil refining Company (BORCO) constructed an oil refinery. All this made Freeport the heavy industry capital of the Bahamas.

Cognisant of all the components of a city needed to be in place to make the city livable, Groves donated land and funds for schools and churches. Some of the churches have recently taken on cathedral proportions. In round numbers there are nearly 100 churches on the island which would work out at about one church for every 450 people.

Early on Barclays and several Canadian banks moved into the central business district. The central area of Freeport originally had the character of a village green but after two supermarkets were built and access was closed to Churchill Square the centre deteriorated into an unhappy gaggle of buildings. Even the magnificent sculpture of Winston Churchill by Marshall Fredericks is lost in the middle of the nondescript buildings.

As tourism started to develop there was a need for an inland attraction and Mrs Ludwig suggested to Groves at a cocktail party in Los Angeles the idea of creating an international shopping centre. Thus the International Bazaar was born. The multi-national replica buildings were carefully crafted by two Hollywood designers Hilyard Brown and Charlie Perron. A Japanese style Torii gate at Ranfurly Circus became the symbol of both the International Bazaar and of Freeport itself. The Port Lucaya complex was conceived in the early 70's and finally completed in the Hayward/St George era. This was supplemented by the oversized Hutchison-funded hotel on the so-called 'Lucayan Strip'.

Signage

The visitor to Freeport may not be too conscious of it today but there was once a strictly enforced signage code. No neon lighting or billboards were allowed, freestanding signs were limited, with a few exceptions, to 15 square feet in area. Now there is a wall at Ranfurly Circus that doubles as a billboard (arguably the largest billboard in the Bahamas) and a retail warehouse with a sign in 10 foot letters reading: THE HOME CENTRE.

(Due to worsening economic situation the 10ft sign has been removed and smaller uncoordinated signs now adorn the building).

Town Planning in Freeport

This subject has been covered fairly extensively in Chapter 10 of the book 'Grand Bahama'. Planning has been in the doldrums for the last three decades of the twentieth century for a variety of reasons so there has been little forward planning. Residential expansion eastwards, subdivision infilling, and a few new industries located in Freeport but most of the expansion took place at the harbour with the Hutchison Whampoa container port and a major ship repair facility. Something that surely needs to be understood by any new management at the Port Authority is the need for an updated Master Plan to be prepared and also for the downtown area to be redeveloped since it has suffered neglect over the years.

Freeport Central Area

Emphasis has been made of the depressed state of the central business district (CBD), particularly Churchill Square. It bears repeating: cities are judged by the character of the central area. Recently a landscape programme was launched for the central area that was certainly a commendable idea but what is more urgent is the total redevelopment of the area possibly with an iconic building that might serve as

Aerial view of El Casino and the International Bazaar. Casa Bahama, once the tallest building in the Bahamas, is at the top of the picture.

symbol for the community instead of the pastiche Torii Gate at the Bazaar.

The civic centre zone north of the CBD includes an impressive Court House that is virtually the first view visitors have of Freeport City. The building has the requisite character for the second city (though of course the fact it was urgently needed at all only highlights the unhappy situation vis-a-vis crime in the community). Though the building is a prominent asset it is unfortunate that site planning and particularly parking was ill-considered. To make an important architectural statement it would have been a good idea to group other government buildings around the Court House. Instead an opportunity was lost when a new large government building was located on a site on the East Mall that it has to share with a fast food restaurant.

I made a thumbnail sketch of a proposal for a Government Civic Centre in Freeport in the classical style. The sketch (reproduced on the following page) shows pedestrian bridges—linking a government multi-building complex. Such a consolidation of government buildings (the Courthouse and National Insurance buildings are already in this location) would make an appropriate statement to underline the presence of the Bahamas government in the Civic Centre of Freeport. It would efficiently keep all the government buildings together and perhaps it just might produce a 'wow' effect. And, at the very least, you would know you had arrived somewhere. In fact new iconic buildings are desperately needed to provide a proper focus to the city. In the immortal words of Daniel Burnham:

>'make no little plans,
>they have no power to stir men's minds.'

A Proposal for Linking the Islands of Grand Bahama and Abaco

Given the close proximity of the islands of Grand Bahama and Abaco—at the nearest point a straight line distance of about 10 miles—and the additional asset of having a chain of small cays between the two islands the idea of linking the two northern islands with a causeway or bridge or a combination of the two has long been discussed. However, because of problems associated with tidal surge and the importance of not impeding the flow of the water in the channel between the two islands it is possible that a more substantial structure than a causeway will be needed. For this reason, we have used the generic term 'transit link' and not 'causeway'. But, whatever the final structure, it is generally agreed that the construction of a link between the islands is not so much a question of 'if' but a question of 'when'.

Dr Morris the respected Bahamian economist clearly expressed one rationale when he wrote: '*linking the major islands through bridges, should forge closer ties between The Bahama Islands. It is an idea some critics have shot down, but I feel confident it could help the long-term economic situation in The Bahamas. These islands will not survive without more direct access. Building and other costs are higher because of their remoteness.*' He might also have added that it gives residents and visitors more choices for work and recreation and most importantly conjoined islands would benefit from scale economies and competition which might be evidenced in everything from the cost of daily necessities, to less expensive capital goods, to less costly governance. Then an imaginative 'overseas' transit link would be a major tourist attraction much like the highway linking the Florida Keys. Such a transit link would spawn much employment in the region. Here are some suggested reasons why a surface transit link makes sense:

- First, there would be many well-paying jobs directly created from the construction of the transit link
- this would be followed by permanent employment of personnel involved in operating the link, together with service, maintenance, security personnel, and so on
- the settlements at the bridgehead (McLeans Town and Fox Town) would receive a major boost to their economies as termini of the transit link
- if a cruise ship mooring facility in eastern Grand Bahama

and a regional airport became a reality, additional well-paying jobs would also become available

- then workers would be required to service the small hotels, commercial centres and residential villages on the channel cays
- this in turn would encourage the establishment of fishing camps, dive operations, eco-tourism, sightseeing and the like
- the access opened up to the channel might also encourage entrepreneurs to look at the possibilities for marine research, fish farming, etc.
- such a link would also be useful to service an energy wind farm which would find an ideal venue in this vicinity

On the subject of cruise ships it is a fair assumption that the cost of fuel will continue to rise and, to remain profitable, cruise ships may seek shorter length cruises. This places Abaco/Grand Bahama in an enviable position. Preliminary observation suggests there are several possibilities for ship mooring sites near McLeans Town. Further, the introduction of a regional airport at the eastern end of Grand Bahama would serve the inevitable tourist developments at the eastern end of the island and, because of the transit link, the airport would serve and encourage development to northern Abaco too. Another potent asset of the project is that the united islands of Grand Bahama and Abaco might help break the metropolitan dominance of Nassau in a way that the current 'anchor' projects will probably not achieve.

At the very least there should be a new harbour at McLeans Town on the Channel side of Grand Bahama Island (this will save a lot of time negotiating the shallows of Sweetings Cay Creek and will allow for deeper draft vessels). This new harbour should be deep enough for a car ferry. And it follows, of course, the harbour at Crown Haven, Abaco should also be improved.

There was a lot more to the report but approaches to government were met with deathly silence. All the people I have spoken to have been equally skeptical, particularly Abaconians, so it is doubtful the matter will be seriously reviewed for several years. I recall years ago when this matter was discussed with Groves he was enthusiastic but clearly understood the time then was not right. He suggested that part of the funding could be paid for by creating luxury islands along the track of the bridge/causeway.

As a postscript to this idea, it is clear the connection of the two islands brings up another aspect of transportation in the Bahamas. It has been mentioned already that the longest distance one can drive in the Bahamas is about 100 miles (from the north to the south of Abaco). Yet the average trip length by private vehicle is probably around five miles and the islands have no hills to speak of and a total absence of snow or ice—all of which would make it a perfect venue for electric

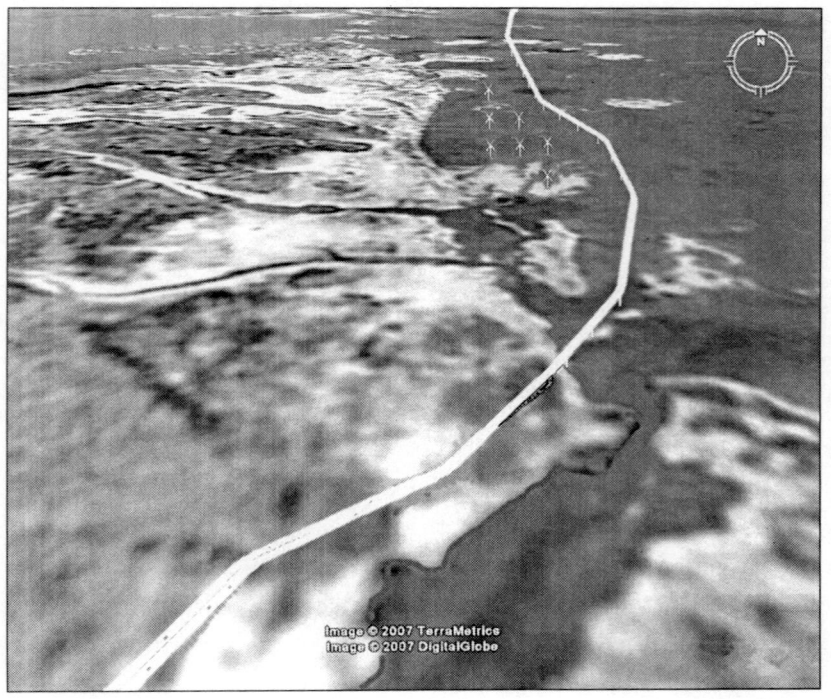

Aerial perspective view of bridge with take-off point north of McLeans Town Grand Bahama. Note the offshore wind turbine farm (photo: courtesy GoogleEarth).

vehicles (ev's). The electricity incidentally could be obtained fairly easily from locally derived wind, solar and tidal power.

It would take a brave government to tackle this problem head-on but, providing there was an economic incentive, it could be an amazing world 'first' for the Bahamas to take the lead in phasing out the personal internal combustion engine. Manufacturers of electric vehicles should be delighted to have a 'test' location like that offered by the Bahama Islands and might even offer the incentives necessary. As a first step the use of hybrid vehicles might be encouraged and even mandated for private transportation, but then, after a transitional period of several years, the only new vehicles permitted for private transportation would have to be propelled solely by electricity.

And this brings me to a personal interest I have concerning ev's. I was awarded a US patent a long time ago for a concept that would extend the range of electric vehicles. My idea would utilize a continuous track (like the third rail of city metros) that would supply auxiliary power and guidance to an electric vehicle without depleting the onboard battery. This rail might be installed between urban nodes such as from an airport to a town centre or, in this case, along the length of the bridge. At either end the electric vehicle would detach from the rail and convert to run on battery power thus considerably increasing the range of the electric vehicle. In time this, or some similar idea, will be necessary to solve our excessive reliance on fossil fuels.

Far out? Perhaps, but if it can be imagined it could just happen. Just remember the immortal words of Daniel Burnham quoted above. It is well to recall that every bridge that has ever been built has created useful, and sometimes invaluable, social and economic advantages and no bridge has ever been demolished without another (invariably more substantial structure) being constructed in its place.

But in all planning, grandiose and otherwise, it is humbling to remember always the Teutonic caveat:

Mensch tracht, gott lacht [man plans, god laughs]

BAHAMIAN FOOD

Pork 'n peas 'n rice is nice
but only if a real small slice
chicken wings and sticky tings
only stomach trouble brings
Johnny cake make belly ache
all deese tings a bit like mud
and help develop de high blood
besides deese tings makum stout
but he who, day in, day out,
only eat dem burger 'n fries...
its sad to say...but he jus dies.

◈

The Bahamas is not the only place that needs to re-consider its diet. The island of Malta currently has the unhappy distinction of having the most obese children in the European Union. Here is how I addressed this situation in verse.

◈

MALTESE P's and FAQ's

The Maltese if you please
eat everything that starts with p's
pasta, pizza, perzut, pastizzi,
pizzelli (and common peas)
—that's not much from plants or trees!
so it's no wonder they're obese
...gastronomic questions please?

PORT & POLITICS

The Bible affords a poetic description of how things happen in the world that seems to be particularly applicable to many periods in our lives.

> For everything there is a season,
> and a time for every matter under heaven:
> A time break down, and a time to build up,
> A time to weep and a time to laugh,
> a time to seek, and a time to lose...
> Ecclesiastes 3:1-8

The Axe Falls

Under the terms of the Hawksbill Creek Agreement, almost unregulated immigration of foreigners into Freeport was permitted providing they were investors or had a job (or the prospect of a job). Clearly this was untenable and the new PLP government quickly abrogated the clause in the Agreement concerning foreign immigration. Though perfectly legal it was contrary to the spirit of the Agreement and new regulation was applied in draconian fashion. It brought about a great change to the social and economic circumstances of Freeport.

A year or so after Independence on the 10th July 1973, a Red Cross Fair was held in Freeport. The administration of the Red Cross had passed from the colonial power to a new sovereign nation. Its new patron was Mrs Marguerite Pindling, wife of the prime minister. I was one of three co-presidents of the local chapter, all of us employees from Port Group companies. When Mrs Pindling came to visit we had a meeting and, predictably, we were told that money was needed to administer the charity and the other co-chairpersons and I, were urgently requested to solicit donations. My first thought was to contact BORCO the oil refinery in Freeport who I knew had had a bumper year. A quick telephone call to the comptroller and I had a pledge of $30,000!

Perhaps you can imagine our surprise when, a few weeks later, all three of us learned that we were to lose our work permits and thus our jobs. The *Freeport News* headline blared in big letters: 'BAHAMIANISATION AT THE PORT'. It was inconceivable to imagine it was a pure coincidence that we three had been selected. It seemed possible it was aimed to send a message from the Ministry of Home Affairs to the Port Authority to open up middle management positions to Bahamians. Ironically though, when all three of us were forcibly retired not one of us handed over our positions to a Bahamian. In my case there was not, at the time, a qualified Bahamian architect/town planner in the entire country. I wish I could say the unpleasant incident of losing the job I cherished was the end of the matter, but it was not. I stayed on because my wife was still working legally though the economy had turned south.

This period in Freeport was fraught with madness. The daughters of the manager of a local bank were kidnapped for ransom. They were soon released but not before the American television networks had aired the incident nationwide. A Swiss chef was on the golf course when he was shot in the head (happily he survived) and a Port Authority's wife was shot in a home invasion robbery. Also about this time we received ominous threatening telephone calls from persons unknown. Though we changed our telephone numbers at last five times, each time we did so the anonymous caller would find the number, sometimes in less than an hour, and offer more threats, in one case, threatening to kidnap our daughter. We, of course, called in the police and the telephone company were most helpful but, even though they tried, they could not trace the call (these were the days before Caller ID). We then did the unthinkable in the Bahamas at this time and employed a bodyguard (interestingly a man who had earlier been convicted of murder!) Later I went to Nassau to speak to a lawyer with connections to the Ministry of Home Affairs. Then, in a matter of days, the calls ceased...

I was not alone of course in loosing my job, many hundreds of non-

> **NATIONAL ANTHEM**
>
> Let's hear a hearty oration for our nation and I don't mean a muttered rendition of 'God Save the Queen'

Bahamians lost their work permits at this time and were asked to leave. It is a forgotten fact that without expatriates—from Groves downward—there would have been no Freeport. It may in fact, have been hardest on the West Indians who were enfranchised as British subjects and voted *en masse* for the PLP and by so doing probably ensured their election in some marginal constituencies. Ironically, they were first to be asked to leave. An organization called FIE (an acronym for Freeporters in Exile) was formed. Despite the fact there was no internet at the time it survived for years. Charles Darraugh, himself in exile, wrote a monthly newsletter mainly concerned with the contentious political and economic scene in Freeport for a year or more.

The immigration situation was so bad at the time that some lawyers were offering advice to expatriates on how to write (groveling) letters to the Immigration Department requesting their Work Permits be renewed. The unofficial policy was that expatriates would be given time to train their replacement (in my case I spent seven years studying architecture and town planning in Birmingham and Cambridge, Mass that was conveniently ignored). In fact, in most cases Permit renewal was denied long before this ruling could take effect.

I should add as a postscript that I have always tried to be apolitical in my adopted country. However, after this incident and when I had the task of acting as a guide for two PLP government ministers in the late 1960's, it has been difficult not to take sides. On two different occasions, while acting as a virtually mute taxi driver, the ministers made many derogatory remarks in my presence about Freeport and its people.

Happily all that is now history. Forty years on, there can be few communities in the world that enjoy the easy racial harmony of Freeport.

Independence in Freeport

Bahamian Independence, declared on 10 July 1973, saw a parade of floats and bands (including the Bahamas Police Band) marching down the Mall. There were many floats and the one constructed by FOCOL was adjudged the winner. I designed the Port Authority float that consisted of a revolving carousel blazoning the header:

"The Grand Bahama Port Authority welcomes this Great Day in Bahamian History"

Towed behind the float was a live band (from El Casino) that played the popular tunes of the day. I did not seek any approval for the caption but I had to wonder if the sentiment of this caption was a shared by the senior members of the Port Authority.

Grand Bahama Port Authority executives (all expatriate white guys!) a little while before Bahamian independence. From the left: George Moore (Airport Company), General William Fisher (Devco), Keith Gonsalves (President-CEO), Martin Dale (Vice-president), Ray Tower (Legal Counsel), Major Bernie Bernard (Corporate Secretary), Ron Golding (Comptroller).

It Is Widely Accepted That We Process Perceived Problems in Five Stages

Let's see how this would play out in the Bahamas on the subjects of **homosexuality** (a ship carrying gays docked in the Bahamas causing a furor)—**religion** (most of the religions in the Bahamas take a fairly literal interpretation of the Bible)—**politics** (for over 25 years one political party has dominated politics in the Bahamas).

The five categories are: denial, anger, bargaining, sadness and acceptance.

First, homosexuality

denial	The Bible says its wrong and that's that!
anger	How dare they visit the Bahamas by ship!
bargaining	Well, as long as they don't tell anybody…
sadness	I feel so sorry for them
acceptance	Well, actually most of them were very nice.

Next, Darwinism

denial	The Bible says its wrong and that's that!
anger	How dare they say we come from monkeys!
bargaining	Well, perhaps God used evolution for his purpose…
sadness	I feel so sorry I insulted monkeys and other animals
acceptance	Well, we are all part of God's great creation.

And lastly, politics

denial	With the PLP there is no need for other parties!
anger	How dare they challenge us in an election!
bargaining	Well, if they play fair at the polls…
sadness	I am so distraught that we lost the election
acceptance	Well, actually we need a loyal opposition

The Thesaurus has another way of putting it: Defiance—rage—haggling—grief—acknowledgement

Incidentally, what's another word for Thesaurus? A circular enigmatic question of course that probably does not have an answer. It reminds one of the Dictionary witticism: 'Circular definition," see: 'Definition, circular.'

An Attempt to Gain Free Publicity for Freeport

After Groves sold out Sir Jack and St George took over the reins of the Port Authority and had to grapple with many problems both political and economic. Sales of land to foreigners dried up and most metrics were down from airline seats to tourism to industrial development. The major bright spot was the entry of Hutchison Whampoa in 1992 to the island and also the many Bahamians into management positions during this time.

The following letter was written in the hope of getting some free publicity for Freeport. If Sir Jack and Edward St George had both been at their most eloquent it could have been a delightful '60 Minutes' segment giving Freeport an incredible public forum. I thought the idea would have been an ideal topic for Morley Safer who seemed to specialize in interviewing British eccentrics. I even sent '60 Minutes' a copy of my book 'Grand Bahama' but alas, the gesture went unacknowledged.

26 November 2003

60 Minutes—CBS
New York City, NY

Dear Sirs:

THE LAST IMPERIALISTS

I would like to suggest there is excellent subject matter for a television segment that might be aired on 60-Minutes concerning Freeport, a private enterprise new town in The Bahamas. The 230 square miles of the 'Freeport Area', Grand Bahama, could perhaps, be considered the last 'imperial' outpost of Empire. It has sometimes been described in the Press as a 'country within a country'. Certainly some of the concessions granted by the Bahamian government to a private company in the Freeport Area are nothing less than exceptional and hark back to similar concessions granted to the East India and Hudson Bay Companies. The concessions were originally granted to a Virginian financier but the company is now headed by two charismatic (but dare I say) slightly eccentric Englishmen as co-Chairmen. Recently the enigmatic Hong Kong multi-national, Hutchison Whampoa, has taken a huge stake (worth approximately $2 billion) in the Freeport venture that is important news in itself.

I think a captivating segment for 60 Minutes could be produced on the subject of Freeport and its principal characters. To give a little background, I am enclosing a copy of my book 'Grand Bahama'. The book does not deal with the present situation in any detailed way but may give some general background on the subject matter. I am convinced there is a great story here and, I think that tactfully approached, the two principal characters would be cooperative and grant amusing and pithy interviews.

I would personally be happy to assist in any way I can. Incidentally, you may recall some time ago you aired a segment featuring Freeport before. It had to do with the immunology clinic.

I look forward to hearing from you.

Yours truly,

Peter Barratt

Sir Cecil Wallace-Whitfield

Cecil Wallace-Whitfield was the Minister of Education in the PLP government. One day I received a strange phone call from Basil Sands the Permanent Secretary to the Ministry asking me if I could visit the Minister in Nassau. I was too dumbfounded to ask exactly what it was about but promised to be at the Ministry offices on Shirley Street two days later.

When I arrived I was greeted most cordially by the Minister and Mr Sands. They explained that they were anxious to improve the standard of education in the Bahamas. (In fairness they had already made great strides in public education under the PLP administration). After a while they got to the point. They asked me if I would relay to Wallace Groves a request to do more to help the cause of public education in Grand Bahama. Is that all, I thought? There were no demands only a polite request.

I carried the message back to Freeport and of course informed Groves about the meeting. He said naturally enough the Port Authority would help but what specifically did they have in mind? Well the Port in course of time allocated land for more schools but, as far as I know, no specific requests were made.

At a recent tribute in his honour Minister Kenneth Russell (who hails from McLeans Town) noted that if it had not been for Wallace-Whitfield the FNM would not have had the strength to stand against the "forces of evil" as he put it. "Whether you believe it or not, many of us were afraid to come out to be counted as FNM's until Sir Cecil made that voyage from the PLP podium after his speech and walked down through that dumbstruck crowd and left the convention. Many of us that night realized that we too were free to speak our minds and do what we felt was best for our country."

Carl Bethel, served as guest speaker for the event and later told The *Freeport News* that throughout the 1970s a myth was perpetuated that if you went against former Prime Minister Sir Lynden Pindling, you were politically dead. 'It was the people of Grand Bahama who had the courage and determination to reject the PLP and return Sir Cecil to the House and resurrect the FNM," he said.

Cecil Wallace-Whitfield died all too soon but as a measure of his services to the country he was awarded a knighthood and as tribute to his service to the country he served, his portrait is included on Bahamian bank notes.

Saving Freeport

The first thing to do when you are shoulder deep in a swamp full of crocodiles is to admit you are in trouble. No one today in Freeport surely denies we are all in trouble. The hurricanes that hit Grand Bahama did not help but there are more deep-seated ills than ill winds. Freeport is one of a handful of company towns in the world and the Freeport 'company' is largely dysfunctional. Just look at what has happened recently.

For about five years a battle has raged over which titled family is to have the larger share in owning the place. Yes that's right, 'owning the place'. Two families own most of the assets of a city valued at around $200 million. In the twenty-first century such a situation is a mind-boggling anachronism.

Litigation is everywhere: The daughters of Edward St George's first marriage threatened to sue Lady Henrietta (St George's wife) and the Port Authority because they claimed their trust fund money had been used to purchase St George's shares in the Port, then St George's wife by a second marriage came down from New York with her lawyer claiming she had dower rights of 50% to the St George estate, then Sir Jack claimed that he and St George's were equal partners only as to dispersement of profits and that he, Sir Jack, was actually beneficial owner of 75% of the shares, then another suit was threatened to sue the Port on behalf of licensees and landowners for "failing to act as a responsible municipal, administrative and development authority."

Since 2004 there has been a very public dispute over the ownership of the Grand Bahama Port Authority. Much of the contentious wrangling has been covered in a (so far unpublished) manuscript entitled: 'The Port at War'. The two titled litigants are Lady Henrietta St George and Sir Jack Hayward. Quite simply Sir Jack claimed he owned 75% of the Port, Lady Henrietta said he did not. There may be something feudal about the situation. It gave rise to the following poem written in 2009:

THE PORT AT WAR

The world over knows about the Port owners' dispute
a matter that to Freeport has brought much ill repute
the actions of both parties—partly motivated by greed
with millions at stake—just how much do they need?
Freeporters contribution to this treasure is untold
for it was they who donated towards this pot of gold
their achievements—now reduced to a mere doodle
make their socio-political status look absolutely feudal.
This matter has dragged on too long to make any sense
Now the dispute is ended, lets revert to the future tense !

And then later Sir Jack strongly criticized the government-appointed trustees for permitting a $12 million dividend to be issued to the 'owners'. Sir Jack contended the money—surely with community support, he noted—should be ploughed back into Freeport. More recently the *Daily Mail* of London featured a spat over inheritance in the Hayward household and quoted Sir Jack, 87, after spending millions of pounds in legal fees finally admitting: 'This is all bloody stupid' (all we have done is to) 'help the attorneys to purchase lovely new homes in Lyford Cay' [an exclusive gated community in Nassau].'

Sir Jack Hayward OBE

One solution to this situation perhaps is to learn from history. In the bad old days of empire, private sector companies carved out great tracts of land overseas and set up an administration of sorts that was profit-driven. In time, the administration became burdensome and inefficient and the central government was forced to intervene. In the case of Freeport the central government might follow precedent and also intervene by insisting the Port be converted to a public company subject to public scrutiny. And, given the special circumstances of Freeport, the government might also specify that a certain percentage of shares be held for Bahamian citizens, it might also recognize that representatives of an 80% majority of the licensees be consulted on important matters as required by the Hawksbill Creek Agreement and lastly it should involve, in a more direct way, the elected members of the Freeport Town Council in the governance of the community. For reasons of transparency government itself might also continue to be a minor stakeholder in the Port.

This poem was written when it seemed as if the legal concept of primogeniture was about to be instituted at the Grand Bahama Port Authority.

PORT LEGACY

Two sirs and a saint
is exactly what they ain't.
We nearly had a peer,
now wouldn't that be queer!
But there's a lady to consider
and a birthright to deliver.

Surely it is almost malevolent
To say books that record, inspire, invent
Must be recent...to be relevant

The ownership row at the Port Authority has dragged on so long it has delayed by at least five years the new revised edition of my book 'Grand Bahama'—but it possibly spawned another publication:

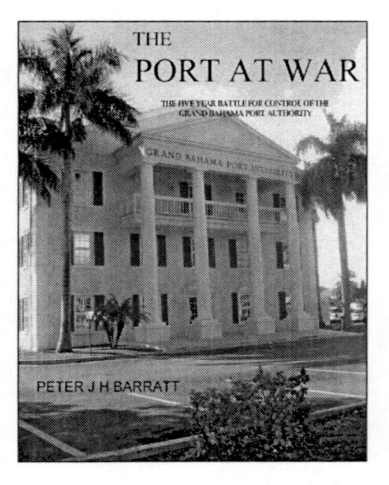

THE PORT AT WAR
THE FIVE YEAR BATTLE FOR CONTROL OF THE GRAND BAHAMA PORT AUTHORITY

PETER J H BARRATT

The cover of a proposed new book about the five year battle for ownership of the Grand Bahama Port Authority

LETTER TO THE EDITOR:

LET FREEPORTERS CHOOSE THEIR FUTURE

The Freeport community is seldom, if ever, asked by the Port Authority Group of Companies for its input or opinion about future development proposals for Grand Bahama. By now we have become a community of sheep, seduced into a somnolent state of acceptance of anything the Port Authority likes to foist upon us. Remember when we were once nearly buried under the biggest pile of coal in the Western Hemisphere? Remember the brouhaha over the harbour by-pass road? Did the Port seek public approval to divert Sunrise Highway where the casino finds itself at the head of a cul-de-sac? Or how about the surcharge to pay for the new airport terminal (now conveniently hidden in the price of our airline tickets)?

Once in a great while, a big developer will try to cuddle up to local residents who are directly affected by development with soothing words and even more statistics—the former, of which, are long forgotten after the project is realized. The Borco refinery immediately comes to mind. Today great rotting cracking towers and tanks scar the landscape—all for less than a dozen years of full production and employment. And now we are in the middle of assessing the cost/benefit of the Tractebel LNG project. We have to hope that history does not repeat itself.

So anyway, just for once, we thought we would make a humble suggestion to the Port Authority about the 'hot' proposal for a new cruise ship facility that kind of 'leaked out' of a speech by Minister of Trade and Industry, Mr. Leslie Miller MP. (note: significantly not a word has yet been forthcoming from the Port Authority).

Now here is one really important issue on which the community should be invited to participate. We presume the Port will not opt for the logical (but costly) alternative of building a new cruise ship harbour. Instead we feel sure they will go for the less costly option of mooring the ships at sea and ferrying the passengers to land. This has been tried before of course—with the Red Boats of Disney—who ferried passengers to Port Lucaya with mixed results. There is surely a lesson or two to be learned here.

If we hope to continue to be a cruise ship destination there are not too many options but, to start the ball rolling, here are a few ideas in no particular order of desirability:

- develop a brand new cruise ship harbour on the south coast in the general vicinity of Fortune/Barbary Beach, such terminal could become the nucleus of a 'new community' that is sorely needed if Freeport is not to be a thousand subdivisions in search of a city.

- locate the cruise ship harbour out of the Port Area at another site near the east end of Grand Bahama where there are excellent beaches and a possible link to Abaco (see this idea expanded later). Many cruise ship passengers are looking for the 'tropical isle' scenario as evidenced by Castaway Cay (aka Gorda Cay).

- develop the north eastern portion of the harbour as a cruise ship terminal, provide a 'Bay Street' experience near to the Fishing Hole, build a new bridge, complete the extension of the Grand Bahama Highway to the airport and develop some sea-oriented facilities on the north coast. Such a proposal might fit well with the 'Moon' project. And the proximity to the airport is, of course, a big plus.

- leave the cruise ships where they are and construct a new coast road (a kind of West Bay Street) along the south coast to link up to Bahamia. Such a proposal, though it will be difficult to sell to the local people, would actually be a bonanza for the small Bahamian communities of Pinders Point, Lewis Yard and Hunters.

Any or all of the above ideas may be rubbish but at least, just this once, let's hear what the people of Freeport, think.

The letter invoked no response. The Moon Project noted above was a bit of a boondoggle, big on audacity, small on realism. A decision was finally been reached to site the cruise ship port at Williams Town in 2009. Clearly not one of the suggested alternatives but since then nothing has happened and according to a government minister speaking in 2011 it is unlikely to happen any time soon.

It has been difficult to be apolitical all the time as the next poem illustrates.

BAHAMIAN POLITICAL DOGGEREL

The challenge threatened 'bend or break',
the result of which was hard to take.
A whole generation of one party rule,
economic downturn and corruption cruel
bribes, property edicts, and drug related crime,
'Country for Sale' blared the news head line.

And then in nineteen ninety two
a new option came to view.
A stalwart new voice from north Abaco
opposed the political *status quo*.
two terms and the country turned around
corruption erased and economy rebound.

And then at the polls a hiccup, so to jest,
the newcomers came out second best.
Then followed another five year session
of bad politics, hurricanes and recession
Another five years of similar effects
broken promises and 'anchor' projects

And now in year two thousand ten
recession bites and things look barren.
But the stalwart man's steady reaction
knows the times call for decisive action.
So, with God's help, the ship of state,
will sail again soon, at a clipper rate.

LETTER TO THE EDITOR:

TELEPHONIC ETIQUETTE

We Bahamians may have some of the worst telephone etiquette in the Western World. I am sure you know what I mean. How often have you telephoned a business to have the phone answered by someone whose tone of voice suggests that she or he (but usually she) has been stirred from sleep or is having a row with her boyfriend and is either hostile or totally disinterested in talking to you. The distant voice grunts, "Yes..." Often there is no identification of the company or office. "Is Mr. Grant in?" you ask. "Err... I'll check." Why check, you wonder, when he is sitting 8 feet away from you on the other side of a piece of glass! Three minutes pass. "You wanna speak to him?" You try not to feel exasperated—why did I call if I did not want to speak to him? "He on the phone." Trying to sound polite you ask, "any idea how long he will be?" Answer. "No." "Alright then I will try later" you say as the phone is clicked off before you finish the sentence.

Bigger offices like to put you on hold. There you are bombarded with messages about what a good company they are or you are treated to a miscellany of scratchy music that probably isn't your taste. All the while you are being told 'how important your call is to us". Really? Many government departments are among the worst at telephone etiquette. In the old days civil servants used to end their letters with "I am, dear sir (or madam), your obedient servant". Wow has that mentality gone forever! And have you noticed how some lawyers have adopted the American habit of getting their telephonists to the answer the phone by saying, "Law Chambers..." What help is that? Are they subtly trying to tell you that they are only lawyer in town worth using? And the person-to-person calls one can't fail to hear in the street and even in enclosed spaces are even more trying. First the callers raise their voice to a shout. A yelled "Hey..." is the usual greeting. From here on much of the talk is in unintelligible street jargon though they seem to be talking a lot about an acquaintance with the initials MF.

And don't get me started about voice mailboxes! People spend their whole day 'being away from their desk' or 'on the phone'. You try to leave a message to be met with the response, " this mailbox is full." If you are not disconnected by now you can try to speak to the operator (the automated voice calls the person an 'attendant'). Try clicking the phone and you will definitely get cut off. Occasionally 'O' works. This gets you back to the 'attendant' telling you to dial the extension number. Of course you don't know it. "Try our alphabetic menu," the canned voice suggests. The problem with that is that dialing systems are alpha-numeric. The Grand Bahama Port Authority has a neat variation on this. If you place a call to an executive the call is immediately directed to his (or her) voicemail and a smug voice cuts in and says, "this person does not subscribe to this system"... and you are promptly cut off.

Bahama Blue (still on hold)

A DEMON TO EXORCISE

Bend or break—the PM decreed
and the city was rapidly on its knees
and so for one long generation
the unhappy result was stagnation.
Then hurricane followed hurricane
a maelstrom of wind and biting rain
creating a cauldron of airborne hell
in which power and utility lines all fell,
followed by tidal surge, and now,
at the Port Authority, a mighty row
of who will receive the mantle
(and the amply funded capital)
of the aged and anachronistic firm
all giving warning clear and stern
a demon must be exorcised to restore
hope, prosperity and peace, before
is reinstated, the happy state of yore.

LEAN MEAN RASTA RAP

Today man its all about youth
that so-called adults call uncouth
other dudes we're out to cream
yeh man, then just dump them clean
were about being loud and mean
and of course we like to be seen
man, that's the way its always been
you know its all about youth
ain't that the truth,
ain't that the truth !!!

POEMS

BAHAMIAN PROVERB:

You woo and flirt, for sweetheart's sake
but all you done is fatten frog for snake

Poetry nowadays is of course out of fashion. In Victorian days people avidly awaited the latest works of poets, indeed some poets were almost treated like today's rock stars. Ironically today in some third world countries people who might be considered technically illiterate can recite many more pages of verse than their first world neighbours. Today poetry in the West has largely migrated into pop song lyrics and, with some exceptions, the lyrics are not terribly good poetry. It is the music that mainly creates the mass appeal. One exception may be rap that relies more on clever rhyming phrases than on musicology. The themes in rap are often anti-authoritarian, anti-establishment.

> **When the ocean fence you in**
> **it's an open invitation to sin**
>
> A variation on a poem by Susan Wallace

Cats are quite lovable. When the St Georges were new in Freeport, Mary, his then wife, asked me if I could identify a site for a building for stray cats but somehow the idea got sidelined. The St. Georges had a tribe of black cats and they donated one of them to us that we named Cuchkin (Maltese for 'dopey'), we paired this cat off with a white one we called Zokra (Maltese for belly button). Following this theme, our present cats are Shizmu (Maltese for 'what's his name?') and Zyra (Maltese for 'little one'). Jerry and Cathy Coleborn have two beautiful Technicolor ex-strays that make up the Ram Rat Pack: Saffron and Lily who have become our special friends. Then there are the two Oriental cats we have we have adopted in London with the unlikely Mexican names of Popocapetl and Mexcal.

Here is poem about these lovable animals:

CATS

Cats like quicksilver in magic flight
are like the tiger in the night
they disappear, appear, embellish
a burning bright vision, then they vanish
but later the stealthy feline sinner
casually returns, at six, for dinner.

MY NEIGHBOUR

It's ten in the morning, "Good evenin'" she say
not to correct her I just mutter "Good day"
"Precious Jesus wid me did just talk…
may God keep you from de devil fork"
(and she's not done with homilies by
a long chalk)
"Praise God" she say, then continues her walk,
ten paces away she continues her prayer…
"an' God keep ya alls in His great and good
care…"

TO THE MAN WHO STOLE MY WALLET

You sir, may never read this ditty
which for the sake of justice is a pity
I really shouldn't call you a swine
But it's the best word I can find
…'to rhyme with 'rhyme'

ENTRAPMENT

Lift up your heads to the rising crime rate -
Bahamaland. This cancer now imperils the state!
A cure may be to draw the criminal element
out of the shadow into the open by entrapment
Perhaps it's not a nice thing to conceive
But it's a better alternative than crime, I believe

◆

5 W'S AND AN H

Not erry body know 'bout dis ryming ting
o' soun' advice writ by Rudjer Kipling
Tis a such pity, since it a very clever ditty

◆

I keep six honest serving-men
(They taught me all I knew);
Their names are What and Why and When
And How and Where and Who.

With apologies to Rudyard Kipling

◈

A LITERARY TRUISM:
originality is the art of concealing your sources

◈

OPPROBRIUM

Sip sip is the medium for rumours to thrive
and treacherous if reputations are to survive
Muddasick is a common forum for complaint
A moan 'bout tings that wrong or simply…just ain't
To survive either opprobrium you will
… need to be a SAINT

PINE RIDGE

The ghosts of Pine Ridge linger still -
community gone, the railway and the mill.
Some planted vegetation, rubbish, fill,
a ruined church and foundations remain, where
other evidence of human habitation is rare

All providing elusive evidence still today
of a vibrant community long gone away,
a record not so much of a physical location
but more about an historic situation
in the pantheon of this island nation.

Dedicated to the one time resident of Pine Ridge.
The Hon. Hubert Ingraham, prime minister of The Bahamas.

Aerial view of Pine Ridge community now completely erased

FREEPORT ARRIVAL

kerrrump...
wheels hit runway
baggage here? yeh!
'...just three day'
'have a nice stay'
keep left and...
we're on our way

right flank
Freeport News
parochial views?
Royal Bank
Port HQ's
left flank
KFC—a bank?

Ranfury Circus
where's the clowns?
Mary Star
Is it far?
domed shrine
whose inside?
doesn't say
'have a nice stay'

Medica Ross
like a shop
bumps...the taxi jumps
hey not too fast!
we're here at last
need to pee, strain to see
ahah!...a turquoise sea!

LAWYERS

Lawyers from time immemorial have been the butt of jokes. I turned one of the most common of them into doggerel with a home town twist:

◆

If you think time is always cheap,
just hire an attorney...and weep

◆

The problem with lawyers:
you never know where they stand
sometimes they represent angels—
sometimes the damned.

◆

Honesty is the best policy, this makes sense
but insanity is an infinitely better defence...

◆

A common definition of gossip:

Hearing something you like about someone you don't.

ECONOMICS

A poverty/rich index from the early 2000's

The haves
The have nots
And...the have yachts

That was 2006. Since the 2008 crash more sober epithets are in vogue. This was from *Marketwatch*:

Two decades of cheap money helped turn Wall Street over to the traders. That led to a very different way of doing business. Wall Street's new culture can be summarized in one powerful quote: "With a trader, the goal of every minute of every day is to make money ... so if running the economy off the cliff makes you money, you will do it, and you will do it every day of every week." Wall Street's culture is without a conscience, reveling in $100 million profit days. Traders act like cocaine addicts. Their brains have warped Wall Street's ethics so badly they can't think of anything but bonuses. They've lost their moral compass.

LETTER TO THE EDITOR:

26 June 2006

FREEPORT ECONOMICS 101

After three natural disasters and an unfortunate business downturn it is indisputable that Freeport has temporarily fallen on hard times. But if we look to our history it can be seen we already have a business model as to how to get development moving again. The early days of Freeport 1963—1970 demonstrated very clearly that a fairly open policy regarding the immigration of foreign entrepreneurs provided a dynamic 'mix' of commercial and professional businesses that, in their train, brought capital, expertise and jobs. Incidentally an important element of the original business model was that licensees in new fields were given (undocumented) assurance that their ventures would remain exclusive until their businesses were established. The introduction of foreign entrepreneurs was a seminal example of the working of the Adam Smith's concept of the 'invisible hand' subtly providing the needed diversity to the industrial base. The downside to this was of course, the feeling that local people were being pushed out by foreigners. But in fact, with the benefit of hindsight it must surely be agreed, it happened less frequently than we imagined. If the concept were to be adopted again, because there are now more qualified Bahamians, fewer foreign entrepreneurs would be needed. But, in certain industrial and commercial categories, there is still a crying need for immigrants and the capital they bring.

Three hurricanes made mincemeat out of Freeport. Overseas investment clearly would help the struggling economy. This is a bit dated but it invoked Adam Smith to come to the rescue!

Towns and cities are much like nations when we consider their economics. The most prosperous countries generally export more than they import (don't ask about the US, that is a special case!) When we refer to what makes cities tick we generally talk about their 'economic base'. This simply means: 'what industries do they have that earn money from outside the community?' And let me quickly add that tourism is one such export industry though its product is usually referred to as an 'invisible export'. In The Bahamas tourism is our principal export bringing in as much as 80% of our overseas revenue. Other sources of revenue come from natural resources that we export; in the case of Freeport this does not amount to much, but includes marine products, limerock and, once upon a time, lumber. Then other important exports would be the products of our industries like the manufacture of pharmaceuticals, styrofoam beads, ship repairing and even straw work (if sold to tourists) all fall into this category. A final source of exports is in the field of services. The financial services sector, tourism, and some portion of the transshipment via the container port, the professions and transportation would be good examples of this category.

Now if a community did not 'export' goods and services (or 'import' capital) it would remain static or, more likely, because there are nowadays more births than deaths, it would regress. A community like Freeport therefore needs to constantly export goods and services and grow its tourism potential. To increase tourism is an obvious aim but the tourist industry is fickle and does not provide very many well-paying jobs. This is why economists are always talking about diversifying the economy. But how? Well the most important resource is our people and after that comes our beautiful natural environment. An educated, skilled workforce creates entrepreneurs who start new businesses, invent and innovate. But that assumes they have, or can obtain capital, to start up new businesses (more about this later). Our natural environment brings people to enjoy our 'sea, sun and sand'. Investor's capital that comes from overseas (especially in the form of hard currency) is the easy option but sometimes runs afoul of our national immigration policy. A foreign investor brings in foreign capital but invariably requires work permits for himself and sometimes for other foreign workers. Is this such a bad thing? Let us consider this for a moment.

In the old days foreign investors applied for and were granted licenses by the Port Authority to open a business when there was no similar business in existence. Unquestionably it was these early investors who provided the bedrock of the Freeport economy. Today the foreign investor has also to seek government approval and generally has to prove that his business is export-oriented and is in an area that is not in competition with an existing Bahamian business. Having satisfied these conditions and demonstrated the proposed business earns a significant proportion of foreign currency and employs Bahamian workers what has been lost? The answer quite simply is 'nothing'. The new investor pays for local goods and services that have a 'multipler effect' (meaning that every dollar spent benefits the community several times its original value). Even if the foreign investor were to repatriate all of his profits (which is most unlikely) the business would still benefit the local community and The Bahamas as a whole. And, in the particular case of Freeport, the business may eventually end up in Bahamian hands due to the so-called 'trickle down' effect. Many businesses in Freeport were started in this way and were later Bahamianised—the *Freeport News* among them.

Now lets take the case of a Bahamian who at the same time as the foreigner in our example is granted a licence to open a small business in a field that already has many similar businesses (a convenience store for example). Which business aids the economy the most? Paradoxically it will almost certainly be the one owned by the foreigner. The reason is that the foreign investor first pays for work permits (a tax by a different name) that goes directly into the Public Treasury. Then, he brings outside funds into the community whereas the Bahamian business may borrow from a local bank, diminishing the amount of seed capital available to other more productive Bahamian businesses (see note above). Then, the foreigner sells his services or products probably to more foreigners than to Bahamians thus earning much-needed hard currency, the Bahamian on the other hand, may cater primarily to local clientele. Indeed, since the Bahamian is entering a business in which other Bahamian-owned businesses are competing, they are now all taking home a smaller piece of the same pie. No community ever got rich by taking in its own washing.

    The moral of the story perhaps is that we still need specialized forms of foreign investment and, if the recent history of Freeport is any guide, the foreign businesses will anyway, in time, devolve to Bahamian ownership.

Adam Smith Jr.

Submitted by Peter Barratt (Editor please use nom de plume)

In the market don't fret
to buy, sell, hold or bet
the trend is your friend

CREDO FOR A GOLD BUG

"We hold what we hold
out of fear of the future
not out of love for gold"

◆

Buy on the rumour,
sell on the news.
Two views,
you choose…

◆

If you want your ill-gotten gains to last
For insider traders: don't steal too fast!

◆

the colour of quiescence is gold
but red for 'iffy' equities unsold

◆

Another aphorism from Germany:
Beim Geld hört die Freundschaft auf.
[Friendship stops with money.]

PERSONALITIES

Another person well known in Grand Bahama from these early years was Doug Silvera. To local people he needs no introduction. I wrote a tribute for him when he passed his 70th birthday that may give a small insight into the man for those who do not know him:

Douglas R. Silvera

When Freeport was just a spewling infant, Doug and his ever supportive wife Pat were involved in helping create a community in a wilderness. In fact perhaps not too many people know he and Pat lived in a trailer parked along Government Road because there was so little housing accommodation at that time. It had another function too...it was his office. Throughout his life Doug has never been far from his work. It is a tribute to the man that Wallace Groves, a man who did not suffer fools lightly, chose him as a confidante. Doug was a vice president of the Port Authority in the difficult early years when the success of Freeport was touch and go. Doug had another great attribute he was a 'hands-on man'. He could operate all kinds of heavy equipment. He often drove a bulldozer, he could operate a dragline (and did so all night on more than one occasion) and when the *MV Freeport* arrived at the harbour on her maiden voyage, he operated a forklift vehicle to maneuver a gang plank into position to the delight of the pitching shipload of passengers and an anxious on-shore reception committee. He received a great ovation for his effort. But his principal physical monument are probably the construction of most of the roads of the island.

There is hardly a lineal foot of road anywhere which Doug has not contributed to planning, clearing, grading or paving. But Doug's talents have not been exclusively employed to his work. I have heard him say that some of his happiest days were when he was a member of the early Prince Hall Lodge in Grand Bahama. And can anyone forget when he won the Bahamas 500 powerboat race? He is also an expert aviator with an unblemished safety record. Doug is a pretty fair golfer too and, unique among men, helped build most of the courses he plays on. I wonder how many people know he even designed a championship golf course in Tehachapi, California! And his fantastic career has not only been on this island.

He once worked for the Kaiser Corporation in Jamaica. He did a stint in road building in Clay County in northern Florida and even built a trunk road in Saudi Arabia...yes Saudi Arabia! There is a lot more that could be said about Douglas Silvera I am sure, but for me I can think of no greater tribute to this giant of a man than that he is someone who always shares his wisdom and concern with all around him. Douglas R. Silvera, a Grand Bahamian icon.

In the long running dispute over the ownership of the Grand Bahama Port Authority Fred Smith QC was counsel for Lady Henrietta St George, one of the litigants. Hardly a day passed that he did not make a statement to the newspapers or issue a news release on behalf of his client. The Court finally found in favour of his client on the matter of ownership and later both parties came to an understanding. Smith is a fervent human rights activist.

In the Bahamas great strides have been made in civil rights. Besides the critically important shift to majority rule, women have also benefited greatly. There has been a female Governor General, a female deputy prime minister and many women governmental ministers. They

Fred Smith QC

Counsel for Lady Henrietta St. George.

are also well represented in the professions, business and the church (though there is still scope for improvement in the two latter categories). Robert Burns writing nearly two centuries ago was prescient enough to know that change was necessary as is evident in the following, slightly abridged, poem.

> "While the world's eye is fix'd on mighty things,
> the fate of empires and the fall of kings;
> while quacks of state must each produce a plan,
> And even children lisp the Rights of Man;
> Amid this mighty fuss—just let me mention,
> the Rights of Women merits some attention."
>
> After Robert Burns

The following was a eulogy I wrote for one of the best friends I have ever had.

SADLY LOST TO THIS WORLD—
THE HERMIT OF LOST BEACH

What we today call the 'hermitage' on Petersons Cay Beach owes its name to Father Gerald Groves the former Trappist monk who sadly died on the 4th March 2003. Father Gerald was the last inhabitant of the building that was originally built in 1902 as a Baptist Church.

Fr. Gerald was born in St. Louis and entered the strict Trappist Order at the Monastery of Gethsemani in Kentucky while in his early twenties. For nearly twenty years according to the rules of the Order he seldom spoke. But he did not see this as an imposition indeed it helped him hone his skills to develop a prodigious memory and he became a respected Latin scholar. His existence in silence did nothing to curb his sense of humour either, indeed he was fond of playing practical jokes on his saintly companions. One fellow monk and kindred spirit who lived in an adjacent cell was Thomas Merton who became a famous author. Later they both were to embrace the hermitic life and leave the monastery. Merton eventually travelled the world and sadly died in an accident in Thailand.

Fr. Gerald after a short residence in Martinique came to the Bahamas where he had lived briefly as a boy.

Around 1960 he was invited by the Catholic bishop to take up residence at the hermitage at Cat Island. The accommodation was small for his six-foot plus stature so he decided to look elsewhere. Father Bruno, the then Catholic priest in Freeport, suggested he look at the old Baptist church on Lost Beach now called Petersons Cay Beach. Father Gerald, saw the place and imme-

Trappist monk Father Gerald with the Hermitage in the background

diately said he would like to move in. The roof was in bad shape and there was no plumbing but a Freeport contractor generously provided men and materials. A short time later Fr. Gerald moved into the 'hermitage' with his two dogs, Moses and Genghis. And all would have been well for him and his hermitic existence if it had not been for the rapid growth of Freeport. Work soon started on the Grand Lucayan Waterway. Roads were cut and tourists invaded his beach. But worse. The developers started to plat the land around the 'hermitage'. Fr. Gerald lost his status as a solitary 'hermit' and drifted away after about six years residence.

From Freeport he went to the University of South Carolina where he gained a PhD. He was invited to join the faculty and became an English literature and Latin professor at the Conway campus of USC. A few years ago Gerald wrote a book called

'Up and Down Merton's Mountain' in which he recorded some incidents of his exceptional life. The book has some interesting insights on his life in Grand Bahama.

Few people today probably remember Fr. Gerald but he was one of those remarkable people that Freeport attracted in the early days. His passing will be a great loss to all those who cherished his great intelligence, humour and humanity.

The Hermitage (formerly a Baptist Church) still standing after half a dozen major hurricanes. This photograph was taken just after the hurricanes of 2004.

THE OLDEST BUILDING IN FREEPORT— A LAMENT

On Barbary Beach over a hundred years ago
Men of faith built a Baptist church you know
With rubble rock and lime mortar locally found
tabby walls, a roof—all construction sound.
So sound in fact, it weathered hurricanes and storms
forest fires, floods and Acts of God in all its forms
But one thing the building could not weather
was neglect by people who should know better!
                                            Anon.

Cecil Hepburn

Hepburn, who no doubt enjoys his role, started by first clarifying some geographical history of Grand Bahama. "The first capital of Grand Bahama was Golden Grove," he stated. "Eight Mile Rock was also capital for a while but West End, which was also known as Settlement Point, became the capital late. In 1949 he recalled he started working for Wallace Groves at the Grand Bahama Lumber Camp. I was a time keeper. He developed a liking for me and talked to me freely. I was asked to go to Whale Cay to be his butler."

As it turned out, Mr Groves, who was campaigning for the approval of the Hawksbill Creek Agreement, actually wanted Hepburn, a de facto leader of the lumber camp workers, to meet with the governor, the Earl of Ranfurly. What used to be a landmark in Eight Mile Rock, Grand Bahama, and located in a two-storey building, Hepburn's Package Store, is now an unofficial academy. Here, retired citizens meet all day every day, to reminisce about past events and experiences. Young people with inquiring minds often stop by for first hand oral lessons in Bahamian history.

The resident teacher is the affable and adept octogenarian Cecil Hepburn. He is one of few Bahamians who played even minor roles in the drama that saw the transformation of vast acreage of Grand Bahama pine forest into what is now Freeport.

When I stopped by recently, what I thought would be a normal chat evolved into hours of story-telling that I could hardly get enough of. I found fascinating his vast inventory of events dating back to the 1930s.

I am grateful to the *Nassau Guardian* for permitting me to reproduce this article By Norman Rolle, about Cecil Hepburn an interesting character who holds court in a dilapidated two-storey landmark building in Eight Mile Rock, Grand Bahama.

Hepburn recalled: "Mr Groves said to me 'I want you to tell the governor the natives of Grand Bahama are pleased that the Port Authority is coming.'" Groves obviously considered necessary such endorsement by the grassroots of Grand Bahama.

Both Hepburn and Groves were pleased with the performance but that would not be the end of the Groves-Hepburn relationship as there was another hurdle Groves had to overcome in order to get government approval to an amendment to the Grand Bahama Port Authority Agreement of 1955. So Hepburn became involved again. Groves needed the support of a second person on the Executive Council who was identified as Charles Bethel, who would stand for reelection to the Assembly and win in the 1956 general election.

He continued, "Then we rigged the election." How was that? Hepburn responded, "I was supposed to run against Charles Bethel in 1956 but, as part of the plan, I did not nominate." I took that statement at face value, but it should be noted that Charles Bethel, first elected in 1943, was challenged only once, in 1949, by William (Willie) Weeks. He was reelected in the 1956 general election and the agreement between The Bahamas Government and Wallace Groves was later amended in 1969 and in 1966 became known as the Hawksbill Creek Agreement in which the government agreed to lease for development to the Grand Bahama Port Authority, 50,000 acres of Crown land.

Cecil Hepburn was born in West End but moved to Eight Mile Rock as an infant. He excelled in the all-age school and became a class monitor. In 1940, at age 16, he relocated to New Providence where he worked as a waiter, first at the Nassau Yacht Club, then at the Royal Victoria Hotel where he became acquainted with several celebrities including Lord Beaverbrook and Count Alfred de Marigny, (the man who was acquitted of the murder charge of Sir Harry Oakes, his father-in-law). The unsolved Oakes murder case continues to receive attention 63 years after.

Hepburn learned carpentry and joinery at Bahamas Woodcraft which was located west of Symonette's Shipyard on East Bay Street. In 1942 he joined The Bahamas Battalion and became a non-commissioned recruiting officer. He also spent some time in Jamaica. In 1945, at the end of World War II, he returned to Eight Mile Rock. A widower, Hepburn has nine children.

Well read and endowed with a sharp intellect, he is engaging and always willing to impart his vast knowledge to all comers. ∎

Cecil Hepburn's quarters in Eight Mile Rock. The building lost its roof in the hurricanes.

Be exceptionally nice to persons literary
For one day, they might write your obituary

I have known Cecil since 1964 when he was a sometime assistant to the redoubtable Major Bernie Bernard at the Port Authority. After I read the article in the Guardian (above) I thought I should visit him. I went to Eight Mile Rock and sat down with him one sunny afternoon in 2006. Showing his age and blind in one eye he was nevertheless very articulate and most willing to impart his vast knowledge to all comers. Here are some notes of my visit.

Meeting with Cecil Hepburn at Eight Mile Rock 29/11/06

We first talked about the early political representation for Grand Bahama. Cecil's memory was in great form. James Henry Young first represented Grand Bahama in 1897 when the population was just over 1000 souls. He served to 1911. Next came Walter Kingsley Moore who served from 1911 to 1935—about the longest term of any serving member—24 years. He was later knighted. (Interestingly in the 1970's a local man of colour from Pinders Point with the same surname, Maurice Moore, represented the island) After Kingsley Moore came James Kelly (there were lots of promotional songs written about him prior to the election that Cecil still remembers!) Kelly surprised and captivated his future constituents on the island by arriving by amphibian airplane from Nassau. He died in 1942. Moore's son ran for office from Grand Bahama but lost to Charles Bethel. Cyril Stevenson (a founder of the PLP) considered a run for the seat for Grand Bahama and visited the island and attended an 8MR church service. He did not however pursue his quest. Willie Weekes who had a hotel in Grants Town also tried out for Grand Bahama but lost out around 1956. This was the same year that Grand Bahama and Bimini became one constituency. In 1962 Dawson Roberts ran and lost to Harold DeGregory.

Cecil also recalled his own life. He married in 10/11/49 and started work 'skinning' logs at Pine Ridge. He noted that the Grand Bahama pine beat out the Finnish pine for pit props because it had more resin and was thus much stronger. His career advanced to aiding with loading ships carrying the pine logs to Europe. He recalls a Cuban schooner coming to pick up high quality pinewood at Mangrove Cay on the Little Bahama Bank. At Groves' prompting he told the Earl of Ranfurly at Little Whale Cay that the people of Grand Bahama looked forward to

Groves plan to develop the island. He recalls when the lumber company moved to The Gap near North Riding Point and the further move to Snake City Abaco. He knew Dr Gottlieb of course. He also met Edward St George when Edward was a circuit magistrate and visited Grand Bahama.

Cecil became, for a time, a chauffeur to Franklin Murphy Chase of the Chase Manhattan Bank in Nassau. Returning to Grand Bahama he supervised loading ships in the harbour and gained Groves respect when he helped arrange for the loading of a German freighter against the advice of three German supervisors. A problem arose though because the Bahamians could not work the winch. He was once involved in striking against the harbour builders when they brought in Okinowan workers. Police were sent to the harbour in force he remembers. In 1962 he acted as labour officer on the Lucayan Beach Hotel project when Diamond Construction were the contractors. He later became the supervisor for the Hawksbill subdivision (Freeport Homes). He was also a member of the Grand Bahama Citizens Committee and acted, for a brief time, as a special advisor to Wallace Groves.

I should add as a footnote he seemed now to be living in poverty and was saddened that he had not been invited to play a more important role recently in Grand Bahama.

Last time I paid a visit to Eight Mile Rock in February 2011 I was told he was seriously ill in the hospital and he died shortly after.

KNOWALL

ears...hear, eyes...eye, mouths...mouth,
but the nose knows

Mr Babak Comes to Town

Hannes Babak

One time president of the Port Authority.

The first time I met Hannes Babak he was fresh off a plane from Vienna with a roll of drawings under his arm. The drawings, prepared by an Austrian firm of architects, were for a high-rise building on Lucayan Beach. These were the grim economic days of the 1980's in Freeport and he arrived fresh-faced with the blessing of the Port Authority to commence a major construction project. But first he had to get building approval and that would entail employing a local architect to ensure that the drawings met the local Building Code. On behalf of a colleague I was one of several architects he met. I reviewed the drawings that were competently prepared except they did not show a secondary emergency exit from each apartment and the elevators for a multi-storey building were seriously undersized. I politely pointed this out but Mr Babak was in Teutonic determination mode and would brook no changes. The interview was quickly concluded.

I should add as a footnote, the building was eventually constructed and, though my colleague was not chosen to act as the local architect of record, the elevators were in fact later re-sized and an alternative egress from all apartments was provided. The completion of the building encouraged Mr Babak to use his entrepreneurial skills to seek more commercial opportunities in Freeport… more about that later (see also the new publication: 'The Port at War').

Hannes Babak was appointed Chairman of the Port Authority shortly after Julian Francis resigned and in no time became the lightning rod between the St George and Haywards camps. Hardly a day went by for months on end without some news about him, his contract with the Port Authority, his work permit, his supposedly conflicting interests and so on. Finally he lost his position with the Port Authority, saw his investments turn south but then presumably sought legal recourse because of his employment agreement. This was resolved through arbitration and it was reported he would receive $10 million from the St George camp and $10 million from the Hayward camp as a settlement. If the payment is ever made he will have done quite well considering the economy has produced so many hardship cases.

Dr Keva Bethel

I need to add a sad note about the passing in February 2011 of Dr Keva Bethel (former principal of the College of the Bahamas). It was doubly sad because her brother, the first Bahamian Anglican Bishop of the Bahamas, died just a week before.

I first met Keva in 1960. With Michael Craton and a few others we used to 'hang out' on the beach on Hog Island every Sunday. In fact we both learned to water ski there. In 'Bahama Saga', with Keva's permission, I used her maiden name—Eldon—for the principal character in my book making the big (but perfectly acceptable 'fictional') assumption that the Eldons were descendants of Read Elding the sometime pirate of mixed race who long ago became acting governor of the Bahamas. Though Keva was a fixture in Nassau her influence as a great role model extended to Grand Bahama and the rest of the Bahamas.

Lost to us but certainly not forgotten.

MISCELLANIA

Sukie is a traditional character in Bahamian folklore. She is generally at odds with the governmen' and she always has her nose in other people's business. Her expostulations are best rendered in the dialect of Eleuthera.

Sukie Ponders Name Changes In Free Port

Sukie say it difficult to keep up wid de name changes in Freeport nowdays.

Take for instance dem two hotels at Ranfurlies Circus.... Ranfurlies Circus you axe? Well dat's de roundebout traffic circle what wuz named for an old gubnor of de Bahamas locate near the Kings Inn, which wuz once call the Princess Country Club and Princess Tower, den de Driftwood, de Sunspree Holiday Inn, Royal Oasis and now it some ting else dat I doan rember. And have you notice what happen to dis property? No man, I don't mean dat million dollar road diversion so dat de developers could provide a beach for the wisitors dat look a lot like a swimmin' pool to me. No, I mean the way it isolate itself from Free Port. A new wall bin construct at the roundeabout that seem to axe you stay away if you not a wisitor. The big wall de biggest billboard in de Bahamas and stop you seein' that Tory gate ting. Once pon a time dat big gate wuz call important symbol of Free Port.

An' what happen to de posh Marrocan-style El Casino? It bin 'christianized' dat's what! The Marrocan dome bin replace by a flat roof. Fancy dat! The two minjrets dat used to look like rockets dem gone, instead dey got some ting on top dat look like garden sheds dough I expec' dey suppose to look like church steeples or some such ting. Dey even got plastic bells man... wit' electronic chimers! Now dat a sometin' hey! Erry hour I tink dey call de faithful Holy Rollers to say der prayers and roll. Well, dem people what use big words say dis all political correct I s'pose. Anyhows it probables seem like a good idea to close de road den, but now the wisitors can't see the Casino now so I guess dem not taking as much money from the Holy Rollers now.

Den der is de 're-label' Westin Hotel that I tink is a bit confudle up bein' part of 'Our Lucaya' dat was once call the Lucayan Beach Hotel (I still tryin' to tink what bit of Our Lucaya is for we?). De glitzy tall glass building shape like a snake is part of 'Our Lucaya' and is also call Westin Hotel. It stan on the gravesite of the ole Oceanus South which once call the Sheraton Hotel den the Atlantik Beach Hotel—dem it blowed up. The ole Holiday Inn once call the Grand Bahama Beach Hotel den Breakers Cay and now, it part of Our Lucaya and it call the Sheraton at Our Lucaya. You understan' all dis? The classy Monty Carlo Casino is be reborned in a buildin' that looks like a large bungelow. I don't tink it will have de same name though. Nex' time I write I will tell' bout you the proper political correct name ...well since writin' dis, it got a name, it call Isle of Capry. We got seven hundred island in de sun and I never heard of one call 'Capry'!

Other tings: de Freeport Inn become the Island Palm Resort. Barcley Bank an' CIBC done join and now Carrybeen someting. Even de light company done gone from being call Freeport Power to Gran' Bahama Power an' Freeport Harbour now Lucayan Harbour.... I doan tink that a good name cos dem Indians was bare naked what paddle canoes. I can't understan' what dey have to do wid a big industry harbour. All dem industry boats scarin' cruise ships away dat bring we wisitors I tink. But, anyways the Gran' Bahama Port Autority ain't change it name yet but I don't tink it have much autority now and it don't control de Port no more, dat all done from Hon Fong.

All dis make de head spin, anyways...dat wat Sukie tink...

Street Names

The original road names in early Freeport followed American antecedents like Sunrise Highway and the Mall (often mistakenly called the Mall Drive). Then of course there is the narrow government-owned road that was once a railway right of way that was grandly renamed Grand Bahama Highway.

Most of the other names in Freeport were selected by Sir Jack Hayward and named for British explorers, pioneers and adventurers (these latter three names were given to three important east/west roads). But Sir Jack must surely have been aware that Nansen and Amundsen were not British but Norwegians! The roads in Hawksbill subdivision were named for Bahamian islands. While the roads in Royal Bahamian Estates were named for islands worldwide. When the Grand Bahama Development Company started its major eastward sprawl there was a need for dozens and dozens of names and so the Development Company, since most Bahamian names had been exhausted, resorted to naming many roads after towns and villages in English counties.

Railway

Strange as it may seem today there was once a very active railway line that ran between Pine Ridge and the Freeport harbour following the line of the present Government Road/Queens Highway. There were also various temporary spurs that were laid down to carry the felled lumber to the saw mills. The history of railways in the Bahamas, and Grand Bahama in particular, has been excellently recalled in a book by Freeporter Darius Williams entitled: "*Railways and Locomotives of the Bahamas*".

Locomotive No. 5 at Pine Ridge before she exploded.

One of the most dramatic events in the history of Grand Bahama before the birth of Freeport was when Locomotive No. 5 exploded in 1949 'with the sound of a thunderclap'. One of the locomotive crewmen was killed. A government enquiry was launched and found that human error was the cause of the accident.

It would have been an incredible tourist attraction to have a railway in Freeport that could have actually carried people from the harbour into town. I mentioned this idea to Groves once and he admitted the railway line could have remained where it was but retaining the line 'never crossed his mind' when he sold the Abaco Lumber Company.

Bahama isle a stately forest boasts
that in times past was lumbered
from coast to coast to coast.
It provided pit prop and plank
earning capital enough to bank
and helped endow a future town.
But without one man of vision
the island would still be forgotten
and Freeport would be unbegotten.

Utopia Limited

Gilbert and Sullivan the acclaimed writers of comic operettas in the late nineteenth century wrote a not-very-successful work called Utopia Limited. It was all about an island colony that tried, not very successfully, to copy the traditions of the Mother Country. It may be recalled due to the influence of Sir Jack Hayward double decker buses, a London Taxi and iconic British telephone kiosks were introduced into Freeport—all of which proved ephemeral. More permanent of course are the British street names and the Union flag gracing the outside of the Port Authority building but that's about the sum total of 'Britishness'.

Krickey… Freeporters don't even play cricket! However I have long thought, with a little tweaking, the G&S operetta could make for a hillarious show (with 'Union' Jack playing in the leading role perhaps!) Here is a verse from the imperialistic score:

Photo of Wesley Butler one of the actors in Grand Bahamarama 1973

This ceremonial our wish displays
To copy all Great Britain's glorious ways
Though lofty aims catastrophe entail,
We'll gloriously succeed or nobly fail!

The show should be a great success but, as for the other intent, I think it would be fair to say it *nobly failed*.

Grand Bahamarama Folklore Show

In 1971 I wrote and co-directed a folklore show that was performed every Monday evening in the ballroom of the Holiday Inn. The other (and more important) co-director and electronic genius was Shelton Archer, a British expat. The show we put together was mimed to a tape and covered the history of the Bahamas from the Lucayans to the present day. It was not great theatre but the young Bahamian cast threw themselves into it with gusto. In fact two of the cast went on to act professionally and one, Willie (Love) Lightbourne, is still around as a popular local singer and tourist guide. The show featured a simultaneous slideshow commentary from screens either side of the stage, live gunfire (in the pirate scene), mist created by dry ice, a holy roller church scene (probably the most popular) and ended with a junkanoo rush through the audience at the end of the show. Jay Mitchell the accomplished local musician was invited to write a song for the show entitled 'Goombay Summer in Freeport'. The last stanza describes the Bazaar:

> Down to the Bazaar you can get what your heart desire
> 'Cos its Goombay Summer in Freeport,
> Freeport/Lucaya
> France, Spain, Africa all the places you want to go
> Between the Straw Market and the Casino
> We even got Mexico!
> 'Cos its Goombay Summer in Freeport.
> Freeport/Lucaya!

The show, including a backdrop beach scene, was taken to Nassau and had a one night stand at the Government High School in front of a few politicians and the governor of the time. We amended the show after July 2003 to include an independence parade. Sadly the folklore show, that had been seen by well over 2000 people, ran its course as actors moved away or became disinterested.

Today there is a great need for something similar to replace 'Grand Bahamarama'. It would help visitors and locals alike to be exposed to the colourful history of this country. It could be a folklore show, a dramatized Junkanoo extravaganza or even a film (possibly even an IMAX presentation). I have tried to get some interest for a screenplay about the Bahamas without success (after all Hollywood produced the highly successful film 'Hawaii' which has precious little history compared to the epic story of the Bahamas). Immodestly perhaps, I even had the gall to suggest that 'Bahama Saga' might be turned into a film script....but everybody I have spoken to is cool to the idea. Not to be diverted I had a copy of the draft of a screenplay dropped off at the BBC in London... (their reply must have got lost in the mail!)

Grand Bahama Museum

The Development Company opened a small museum at the Garden of the Groves in the early 1960's. It languished after Tim Hutton, a Devco employee, left the island. Then, after Groves retired, he and his wife Georgette took over the Garden of the Groves and provided funds to move the museum to a better location with more space and a water feature which was adapted to take the Lucayan human remains of the Lucayan Indians that had been recovered (stolen might be a better word) from the Lucayan National Park. It was not one of my better ideas to collect all the bones together and relocate them in the museum (see the remorseful poem that follows).

The American Women's Club did a fantastic job of administering the museum for many years portraying the history of the island right up to the present day. Indeed, besides the Lucayan culture, there were exhibits featuring piracy, slavery and the lumber industry. And, to bring the historical perspective up to date, there was even a prototype electric car on display that had been developed by a Freeport company. But alas, somebody had the idea that a snack bar would be a more profitable venture and the museum was closed.

In 2007 the 12 acre Garden, devastated by the hurricanes, was taken over by Erika and Ed Gates. Within a year it was restored to its former glory—indeed it was actually improved with a new restaurant, some small shops, a Lucayan village and a labyrinth. There are also lots of water fowl around, a talkative parrot and two great blue herons appropriately named Wallace and Georgette. Since the first museum closed in this location there has been a lot of talk about creating a new museum in Grand Bahama possibly at the Garden of the Groves again.

Seagrape Church

As a graduate of Georgetown University Groves always had a great appreciation for the Church of Rome. Indeed he converted to Catholicism shortly before he died. Right from the early days he was generous to all churches in Freeport donating land and sometimes money. One example of his generosity was to the community of Seagrape. Abaco Lumber owned a parcel of land to the far west of Eight Mile Rock and Groves donated it to the Catholic Church. But this wasn't only a land donation, he offered a $30,000 lump sum as well. It wasn't much money to construct a church building even in those days but I designed a church that could hold at least 70 people. The construction was unorthodox—some say it looks like an upside down boat—and in constructional terms that's what it is. The curvilinear construction gives strength to the structure, the walls and roof being part and parcel of the whole building. Essentially the money went to pay for a roof, not walls. The west end of the building, that nobody sees, is shaped like a bishop's mitre. Incidentally the talented Bahamian writer Keith Russell used the church as a murder scene in his thriller 'When Doves Cry'.

The building is now over 40 years old and has become riddled with termites so without serious renovation it can't have much more life in it.

St. Agnes Church in Seagrape donated to the Catholic Church by Wallace Groves

LETTER TO THE EDITOR:

ARMAGEDDON AND THE BAHAMAS

Armageddon is simply a town in northern Israel called Har Megido that has been the site of a few battles in the past—but it has a more sinister and prophetic meaning. In short it is the Biblical name for the last great battle that brings about the end of the world, yes, that's right, the End of the World! How likely is that? Well actually the answer is— fairly likely!

Consider this...

In fairly recent historic time Jews re-occupied a chunk of land in the Middle East called Palestine that had been in Arab hands for nearly two millennia, (and for the last fourteen hundred of those years the residents of Palestine were Muslim). The explanation for the Jews to return to this territory was that their ancestors lived there two millennia ago. Also the Judeo-Christian Bibles both say that God gave the Jews the land and that in 'the latter days' they would return to this land. One billion Muslims and 700,000 dispossessed Palestinians think this is unjust. For, not only have the new inhabitants of Israel taken land that formerly belonged to Palestinians, they are also continually expanding into what is left of the former land of Palestine and they police the occupied territory of the 'West Bank' (the area of land between Israel

---

Hardly a day goes by without somebody using the word...Armageddon. So what exactly is Armageddon? Above is an unpublished letter on the subject. Armageddon is understandably a frequent topic of sermons in the Bahamas. And it should be. Without doubt it could be a touchstone for a disastrous conflict that might involve Judaism, Christianity and Islam. The recent revolt in the Middle East may—or may not—be a precursor of Armageddon.

proper and the River Jordan). The Palestinians have fought back with guerrilla tactics and are declared 'terrorists' which gives the Israelis an excuse to occupy more land and build more settlements.

Well, why should we care? Quite simply because the United States, our near neighbour and protector, has promised to defend Israel from attack. But soon the Muslims (who already count one country with a nuclear arsenal may soon be joined by two or three others) will inevitably one day feel strong enough to right what they see as a terrible wrong. So conflict is inevitable and, once it starts, the loosing side will reach for its nuclear weapons. In the Bahamas we may not witness the mushroom clouds of Armageddon but we will certainly feel the deadly effect of a world war fought with nuclear weapons.

Incidentally, according to President Carter there are 9.4 million nominal Palestinians of whom 3.7 live in the West Bank and Gaza, 200,000 live in east Jerusalem, 1 million live in Israel and 4.5 million are scattered among other (mainly Arab) nations. 700,000 Palestinians were dispossessed after the formation of the State of Israel.

With this in mind is it any wonder that many commentators suggest this is a formula for a future Armageddon?

LETTER TO THE EDITOR:

MIDDLE EAST

Presidents Carter, the Bushes, Clinton and Obama couldn't do it. Neither could Blair, Mitchell and a consortium of powerful political blocs. Yet an overflowing crowd of largely well-educated but unemployed Egyptian youths started a revolution in Egypt that could, at long last, push Israelis and Palestinians to come to a solution over the festering Palestinian problem. It might finally resolve the illegal settlements situation on the West Bank. And from this perhaps, we might also see an accord on the return of some Palestinians to their former homes in Israel and even an understanding on the future of Jerusalem. ...hopefully the time has come.... *Inshallah.*

I hurriedly wrote letter above (that was not published) in the early days after the unrest in Egypt. After this event I believe the Middle East, where I lived for two years, would never be the same. Despite a lot of dire predictions, the revolution could trigger a lot of scenarios—some even positive for Middle Eastern peace and prosperity. Even the United States has come to realize that automatically backing actions of the Israeli state regarding settlements is neither in its own or Israel's interest. Like their policy towards Cuba, after this event in Egypt, they might find themselves on the wrong side of history.

A popular contemporary Bahamian song inspired this next rhyme.

FAITH

Errybody want heaven
nobody want dead
better words were never said
you see it brings to the fore
home truths you've heard before
once ones dead all is uncertain
what's behind this dreaded curtain?
the funeral pyres a ghostly wraith
so what they tell you is needed...is faith
...more faith

THE PREACHER

He means well of course, but preaches far-out apocalyptic views
and consequently gets tumultuous approbation from the pews.
As for the veracity of his theology, (that some might call abstruse)
it is like most creeds since Christ—they all just pick and choose.

EVER WONDER ABOUT THE COLOUR SPECTRUM?

In 1801 Thomas Young proposed his trichromatic theory, based on the observation that any colour could be matched with a combination of three lights: red- yellow- blue. Anybody nowadays familiar with computer printers is probably knows that when the black ink runs out, the printer can still print in black using the three primaries.

◈

Primary colours are strange fellows
comprised of reds, blues and yellows
mix any two and the secondary's seen
and results in orange, indigo and green
primaries and secondary's mixed
gives hyphenated tertiary colourations (six)
makes sense so far but to the chromatic stack
mix red, blue, yellow—and you get black!

Florida is a near neighbour of the Bahamas and throughout history has interacted with the Bahamas. Only late in the nineteenth century did Miami exceed Nassau in population. Here is some historical background on Florida taken from 'Bahama Saga.'

Historical Footnotes

Florida was British 1763–1784. Then it became Spanish until (1784-1821). It was purchased in 1821 by the United States (in fact if Spain had not agreed to the purchase it would probably have been annexed by force anyway like Texas).

Fort Apalachicola was built by the British in the War of 1812 and garrisoned by runaway Negroes. The Seminoles long enjoyed a trade with the Bahamas.

Robert C Ambrister was a soldier and adventurer executed on General Jackson's orders in 1818 for intervening in the affairs of the Seminoles. Ambrister was born of English parents in Nassau, served with Wellington in Europe and returned to the Bahamas. In the British colonial period in Florida, Britain used Seminoles as border guards. British Governor Tonyn reported 'they were well affected and I can confide in the headmen'. (One Seminole was even recruited in the Royal Navy). The fledgling United States (Georgia and Tennessee especially) was angered at the runaway slaves who were escaping to Florida and intermarrying with the Seminoles (hence being known as Black Seminoles).

In 1819 twenty-eight Seminoles arrived in Nassau and claimed they had been robbed and driven from their homes by the Americans. They had been told that to the rising sun was a land of freedom and used dugout canoes to land first at Red Bay, Andros and Joulters Cays. They were furnished with rations and lodging referred to in official papers'..to relieve their immediate distress.'

Some Bahamians of Seminole ancestry still bear the surname 'Bowleg'. There are, for instance, three entries with the surname in the current Grand Bahama telephone directory.

Angels

I was looking something up on *Wikipedia* about angels and became so interested in the subject I wrote a short treatise (just published) about them. I mentioned the fact to Larry Smith the Bahamian journalist who retorted that I 'did not look like an angel kind of guy!'

Certainly I am not particularly religious but had a good grounding in biblical studies since my older brother was my Sunday School teacher for many years. With this knowledge I received better than average grades in Divinity classes at school (do any schools offer Divinity classes any more I wonder?) After some research I wrote this book in the hope it would foster interest in the biblical studies and provide another interesting viewpoint to the study of the Bible.

This is the cover of the recently published book on the subject of angels

As I note in the book, angels are mentioned over 270 times in the Bible and appear at almost all important biblical events. Besides this, many people in many cultures, believe they are omnipresent in the world we live in. And, as the Christian Book of Revelation would suggest, they may have an even greater part to play in the future. In fact angels, throughout the history of the world, have been very busy undertaking all kinds of tasks for Almighty God. Lord Byron whimsically suggested their functions in a poem:

The Angels were all singing out of tune,
and hoarse with having little else to do,
excepting to wind up the sun and moon
or curb a runaway young star or two.

And here is a simple verse by a lesser poet on the same subject:

ANGELS ON A PIN HEAD

Just how many of the angelic host
can stand on the head of a pin?
Probably a million billion at most
a few less, if the pin shaft is thin.

FUTURE

And Where Now?

Of course there are major changes ahead for Freeport and the nation. There are for instance, only 45 years (in 2010) left for the Hawksbill Creek Agreement to run its course. By 2015 the customs provisions of the Agreement will up for review. A minority of people think the government may take control of the Port Authority before the Agreement runs out.

The fledgling city councils all over the country will almost certainly devolve into something better funded, more democratic and powerful at the local level. It is even possible that the Freeport City Council may one day assume some if not all of the governmental powers of the Grand Bahama Port Authority.

And like it or not, the Bahamas will become more pluralistic. Already there is a substantial Haitian population (documented and undocumented) in the country and that will probably increase. Then people from all over the world who visit or work in the country may, like me, want to live here permanently and become naturalized. We are certainly going to see a large influx of Chinese who will want to physically follow their investments in the country. And, as the Chinese influence increases, so American influence will diminish somewhat following the established principal that power and influence follows money. The Bahamas will probably choose to remain within the Commonwealth, less certain is whether it will retain the British monarch as head of state.

But whatever happens, if Bahamians are true to the patriotic words of the National Anthem we can hold up our heads as members of a proud, respected, free and democratic nation and march on to glory; onward—upward—forward—together.

THE FUTURE

today is knowable, substantial and 'now'
but tomorrow will be the future... wow!

the great unknowable unknown looms
expectation, anticipation, population booms
cherished are memories of times gone by
now what does the future hold and why?
this is when every thing we learned may end
and with a new world, we will have to contend.

INDEX

A
Abaco 11, 48, 50, 97, 99, 100, 118, 150, 156, 161
angels 168, 169
Armageddon 162

B
Babak, Hannes, 150, 151
Bethel, Dr. Keva, 152
BORCO 94, 103, 117
Boyce, Michael, 30

C
Carter, President Jimmy, 80, 90, 91
caves/blue holes 46, 59, 73
Chesler, Big Lou, 20, 23, 27, 34
Columbus 73, 89
CBS (60 Minutes) 108 (onwards)
Courthouse 97
Cuba/Cubans 149, 164

D
Dale, Martin, 16, 17, 106
Devco 23, 30, 43, 46, 58, 155, 160

E
Eight Mile Rock 53, 146-150
elections 71

F
Film Colony/studio 64, 160
flora/fauna 40, 41
folklore/Utopia Ltd 153
Fountain of Youth 7

Francis, Julian, 31
Freeport 3 (onwards)
Freeport News 61, 63, 86, 104, 111, 136

G
Gambling 17, 18, 21, 32-34
Garden of the Groves 160
Grand Bahama 3-13, 15, 16, 19, 20, 23, 32, 36, 43, 45, 4650, 58, 63, 70, 73, 87, 89, 95, 97, 108, 109, 111, 117, 140, 144, 146, 149, 150, 155, 156, 160
Grand Bahama Port Authority(GBPA/Port at War) 14, 16, 23-26, 30, 36, 43, 70, 86, 93, 95, 104, 106, 108, 113, 116, 117, 136, 139, 147, 150, 158, 167
Gonsalves, Keith, 30, 106
Groves, Wallace and Georgette 11, 12, 15, 16, 19-26, 30, 34, 36, 93, 100, 108, 111, 139, 146, 149, 161
Groves, Fr. Gerald (hermit) 142

H
Hawksbill Creek Agreement 13, 19, 43, 103, 114, 146, 167
Hayward, Sir Jack, 15, 22, 30, 46, 93, 114, 151, 158
Hepburn, Cecil, 11, 146 (onwards)
HM Queen Elizabeth II 15
Hughes, Howard, 27-29
hurricanes 49 (onwards)

I
Ingraham, RH Hubert (Prime Minister) 70, 79
International Bazaar 17, 24, 94, 159

L
Levarity, Garnet and Warren, 13
Ludwig, D.K. 20, 24, 26, 94
Lucaya, Lucayan (Indians) 6, 7, 11, 17, 20, 33, 36, 39, 47, 73, 94, 150, 154, 159, 160
Lucayan National Park 5, 46, 48, 49, 55 (onwards)

M
Maathai, Wangari 40
Miami Herald 69-87
Middle East 162, 164
Miller, Sir Albert, 30
Moss, Willie, 30
Museum, Grand Bahama 160

N
Oakes, Sir Harry, 19

P
Pindling, Sir Lynden O. 24, 69, 70, 103, 149, 156
Pine Ridge 11, 93, 130
pine trees 41, 54
Porel, Jan, 93

R
Railway 155, 156
Rainier, Prince (Monaco) 16

S
Sands, Sir Stafford, 14, 34
Seagrape 14, 34
Silvera, Douglas, 30, 36, 139
slaves/slavery 7, 9, 90, 160, 167
Smith, Frederick, QC. 13, 140
St George, Edward, 16, 22, 27, 30, 57, 94, 108, 112, 126, 150, 151
Symonette, Sir Roland, 18, 198

T
telephones 51, 104, 121, 158

W
Wall Street 19, 86, 87, 133
Wallace Whitfield, 111

X
Xanadu 27, 28

A Critique

This is a remarkably original book by Peter Barratt. As he admits in the Introduction one needs an untidy mind for this kind of writing. Certainly a gross understatement. The book starts logically enough with a brief history of the island. He is well qualified to write about this since it was adopted from a talk he gave at Book & Books in Miami introducing his book about the island entitled: *Grand Bahama*. Then Barratt digresses to write about the erosion of the environment on the island. Here and elsewhere he adds a short poem to drive the point home. The book alludes to the disastrous six-year dispute over the ownership of the Port Authority. For a fuller account of this fiasco he is planning to publish a new book entitled: *The Port at War*.

Then we go back to the early days with insightful biographical notes about some of the early personalities. This he amplifies with an insert he calls 'Name Dropping' in which he lists some of the famous, and not-so-famous people who have visited Freeport. Peter Barratt is one the few people left who knew Wallace Groves the founder of Freeport personally. He adds some thoughts about the genius of the man that are generally at variance with the popular conception of Groves. Off on another tack he discusses and the Hawksbill Creek Agreement (the legislation that brought the city into being) and the planning of Freeport. It is a subject he is well qualified to address since he was the Architect/Town Planner of Freeport for 15 years.

Next he has some things to say about economics replete with more poetic truisms. In another detour Barratt includes several poems (he admits some may qualify as doggerel) mainly about the local scene. There are rhymes about turkey buzzards, neighbours, preachers and the Freeport Post Office. A particularly ingenious poem concerns the colour spectrum. Barratt includes an amusing piece written in the Bahamian dialect that features Sukie a character out of Bahamian folklore who is at odds with 'autority' and much else besides.

The hermit of Petersons Cay beach who was a personal friend is described in a heart-felt eulogy. Then, instead of another horizontal diversion, Barratt ascends upwards to discuss angels. It seems he has just written and published a book on the subject entitled: *Angelic Verses*. Predictably he adds a short poem on this subject too. In conclusion Barratt states the book contains some very personal and subjective musings that he thought the reader might find interesting. I think he may be right.

~ L. N.